D0495252

Supporting the prime and specific areas of development

What does it mean to be one?

What every practitioner needs to understand
about the development of one-year-olds

Jennie Lindon

Updated in accordance with the 2012 Early Years Foundation Stage

Contents

03208

Keighley Campus Library
Leeds City College

12\13   10 MAY 2013

WITHDRAWN

Published by Practical Pre-School Books, A Division of MA Education Ltd,
St Jude's Church, Dulwich Road, Herne Hill, London, SE24 0PB.

Tel: 020 7738 5454

www.practicalpreschoolbooks.com

© MA Education Ltd 2012

All images © MA Education Ltd., other than the images listed below. All photos other than the below taken by Lucie Carlier and Ben Suri.
Front cover image: © iStockphoto.com/Imgorthand

All rights reserved. No part of this publication may be reproduced, stored in a retrieval system, or transmitted
by any means, electronic, mechanical, photocopied or otherwise, without the prior permission of the publisher.

ISBN 978-1-907241-39-0

KEIGHLEY CAMPUS LIBRARY
LEEDS CITY COLLEGE

KC03208

Focus on one-year-olds

What does it mean to be one? covers the baby year up to the first birthday and into the year in which toddlers are one plus how many months. A huge amount happens developmentally over this timespan and some babies and toddlers will remain the full responsibility of their own family: parents or other adult family members. However, over the first part of very early childhood, some babies and toddlers will experience the transition into some kind of early years provision for part or all of their week; within a nursery or with a childminder.

The approach and ideas of this book are relevant to practitioners who are working with babies and toddlers anywhere in the UK. However, the structure of the book follows the statutory framework for England of the Birth to Five Early Years Foundation Stage (EYFS). This new edition of *What does it mean to be one?* has been updated following the revised framework, implemented from September 2012. The main EYFS documents can be accessed through the Department for Education website (details on page 54). At the time of writing, Scotland is the only other nation in the UK that has specific guidance about best practice with under-threes (Learning and Teaching Scotland, 2010).

A learning journey across early childhood

In England, early years practitioners have been working within the EYFS since September 2008. The revised statutory framework and supporting guidance are much reduced in length and some details, like the early learning goals (ELGs) for the end of the stage, have been changed. Of course, everyone has to become familiar with the revised framework. Yet, early years provision with established best practice will not need to make sweeping changes to their approach to children and families. The crucial elements of best practice have not changed.

One focus of change is that the six areas of learning from the first EYFS framework have become seven areas, divided into three **prime** and four **specific** areas. This framework is one way of considering the breadth of children's learning. But of course babies and children do not learn in separate compartments; the whole point is that their learning crosses all the boundaries. The overall aim of identifying particular areas of learning is still to ensure that early years practitioners do not overlook important areas of development.

The rational for identifying three prime areas of learning is that secure early development rests upon:

- Communication and language

- Physical development

- Personal, social and emotional development.

These three areas are identified as, *'particularly crucial for igniting children's curiosity and enthusiasm for learning, and for building their capacity to learn, form relationships and thrive'* (page 4, DfE 2012). The order above is the one given in the EYFS framework. I have moved personal, social and emotional development (PSED) to the front of the list for all the books in the *What does it mean to be…?* series. In terms of child development, it makes more sense to start with the crucial underpinning of PSED.

There is a sound developmental basis for arguing that, without secure personal, social and emotional development, toddlers and young children spend considerable energy striving for affirmation that they are accepted and loved for themselves. Concern has grown over the shaky communication skills of some young children, whose early experiences have not supported their development. Children's ability and motivation to be an active communicator – right from their earliest weeks and months – opens the door for other aspects of their development.

Making physical development a prime area is also welcome, since this aspect of how babies and young children learn has often been undervalued. Babies need safe space for movement and toddlers need to have easy opportunities to be physically active; encouraged by adult play partners who do not try to curb natural exuberance. There is good reason to be concerned about the well-being of young children whose limited opportunities for active play have already pushed them into sedentary habits.

The guidance for early years practice is that the three prime areas should be uppermost in the minds of practitioners working with younger children. The age range has not been made specific, although the implication is that this strong focus applies to working with under-threes. The other four specific areas are still of relevance for babies and toddlers. The focus needs to be on practitioners' thorough understanding of how the earliest experiences establish positive beginnings to the child's learning journey in these areas of development:

- Literacy

- Mathematics

- Understanding the world

- Expressive arts and design.

As young children reach three years and more, it is expected that practitioners will focus their attention more evenly across all seven areas. However, throughout early childhood practitioners need to be very alert to the prime areas, as the basis for successful learning within the four specific areas. If young children are struggling within one or more of the prime areas of development, then the main focus must be that: on identifying the nature of the problem and how you can best help children, in partnership with their family.

Early Education (2012) was commissioned by the DfE to produce the supporting non-statutory guidance across the Birth to Five age range. This document explains the four main themes of the EYFS: A Unique Child, Positive Relationships, Enabling Environments and how they contribute to the fourth theme, Learning and Development. The guidance also includes a revised version of 'Development Matters', cut back in line with the much reduced number of early learning goals (ELGs) for the end of the EYFS. This material offers ideas about how supportive practitioners behave with babies and children and what they could provide within the learning environment. These suggestions should refresh and inform best early years practice. They are not a have-to-do checklist.

The document provides some developmental highlights for children's journey towards the early learning goals. This resource continues with the previous EYFS' approach of broad and overlapping age spans: birth to 11 months, 8-20 months, 16-26 months, 22-36 months, 30-50 months and

40-60+ months. The developmental information is a reminder of the kinds of changes likely to happen, if all is going well with babies and young children. They are, for instance, a brief reminder of the early part of the learning journey towards literacy or numeracy. The items are not an exhaustive list of everything that happens.

As with the first EYFS framework, these developmental highlights and linked practical advice were neither developed, nor intended to be used, as a checklist to assess children. Their value is dependent on the secure child development knowledge of practitioners using the resource.

The aim is to refresh realistic expectations, supporting practitioners to focus on the uniqueness of individual babies and children and to protect time for them to enjoy secure learning over early childhood. There should be no headlong rush to get any under-threes, let alone babies, into the 'older' age spans. Managers and practitioners all need to understand that none of the descriptions, with the sole exception of the ELGs, are required targets to be observed or assessed.

Child-focused observation and assessment

The revised EYFS continues to highlight the importance of ongoing observation, which enables practitioners to shape learning experiences that are well-attuned to the interests

and abilities of individual babies and toddlers. The revised statutory framework stresses that much of this observation arises within day-by-day alert looking and listening. Some practitioners call this informal or incidental observation and sometimes, not always, it may be captured with a brief written note or a photo.

All children should have a reliable and descriptive personal record, which will include some more organised observations. The revised EYFS gives very clear direction that the process of observation and assessment, 'should not entail prolonged breaks from interaction with children, nor require excessive paperwork. Paperwork should be limited to that which is absolutely necessary to promote children's successful learning and development.' (page 10, DfE 2012)

The situation continues to be that, except for the EYFS profile, there are no statutory written formats for observation and assessment, nor for any kind of flexible forward planning. Early years settings and childminders can continue to use approaches that have worked well so far. The only difference is that layouts will need to be changed in line with the seven areas of development. Established best early years practice is not challenged by the revised EYFS framework.

Attentive and knowledgeable key persons will continue to be aware, and keep some records of, the progress of individual babies and toddlers over time. Observant practitioners will learn from watching, listening, being a nurturing adult and play partner to babies and toddlers. These observations, often acted upon but not written down, will make a difference to the detail of what is offered to individuals and to sensible short-term changes in planned opportunities for a very small group of toddlers.

Flexible, forward planning will continue to be responsive to the needs and interests of individual babies and toddlers: through continuous provision (the learning environment) and flexible use of interesting experiences that need a bit of adult forward planning.

The revised EYFS still applies until the end of the reception year at which point children are assessed through a revised EYFS Profile. The total number of ELGs has been significantly reduced: from 69 to 17, with some different wording. All the ELGs apply to the end of the phase of early childhood: specifically to the level of progress expected by the end of the summer term of the academic year in which a child reaches five years of age. It would make no developmental sense to attempt to apply any ELGs to babies or toddlers.

Two-year-old progress check

The revised EYFS has introduced a new element to the statutory requirements for early years provision. From

September 2012 there must be a descriptive individual assessment within the year that children are two: a two-year-old progress check focused especially on the three prime areas of development. All early years provisions with two-year-olds must organise this developmental assessment, by the key person.

The Early Childhood Unit of the National Children's Bureau (2012) was commissioned to produce non-statutory guidance to support undertaking this statutory assessment. The document 'A Know How Guide: the EYFS Progress Check at Age Two' explains the nature of the check, principles of good practice and a few examples of how the check might be done. These are possibilities and not required *pro formas*. The statutory EYFS framework does not require a set written format for the two-year-old check.

Usual good practice for ongoing observation of toddlers and rising twos should inform much of the two-year-old progress check. This assessment is ideally to be completed soon after the second birthday, timed to dovetail with the two-year-old health and development review made by health visitors, as part of the Healthy Child Programme.

You do not have to change existing records for toddlers that are currently working well, but amend to include the seven areas of development that affects all record keeping from September 2012.

Nurseries and childminders who have taken responsibility for the twos since they were babies or young toddlers, will have descriptive information as part of the records, which are already shared with parent(s). Existing best early years practice should have established a pattern that any written observation includes examples to support the assessment of existing skills or concerns. These descriptions will highlight what this child likes, perhaps dislikes and his or her particular interests within play, personal and daily routines or social communication.

Nurseries and childminders who enjoy the advantage of a longer relationship with families from babyhood or the toddler year, will have established a communicative partnership with parents. The pattern should have been developed of highlighting this baby's abilities with a can-do focus, yet with an honest conversation about any concerns, even from within the baby year. The two-year-old progress check has been made statutory because children are more effectively helped when any problems are identified at a young age and addressed. Of course, practitioners involved with babies and toddlers do not postpone important conversations with a family until the new progress check.

Child development

The effectiveness of any kind of assessment over early childhood is highly dependent on the key person's child development knowledge. Practitioners must have realistic expectations for babies or toddlers. If practitioners' child development knowledge is stronger for over-threes, then there is a risk that under-twos can be judged as not doing much at all. Communication, thinking, concentration, playful exchanges or other important developments fail to be recognised in the baby or toddler version.

The learning journey of early childhood starts with babies – in fact research into brain development prior to birth tells us that even newborns have already been learning in the womb. Infants are poised to go; they are not a blank slate.

However, the misleading message is often that 'babies are boring' or 'they don't do anything' or 'they don't start learning until…'. It is crucial that practitioners working with babies and young toddlers are alert to very early learning. For instance, that babies develop essential communication skills long before the first recognisable words or that they have growing knowledge and understanding of their own world.

Sound child development knowledge can be supplemented by the 'Development Matters' guidance materials mentioned on page 3. These developmental highlights are intended to remind and provoke further ideas about what you may have noticed and pointers for what you could be alert in your daily practice.

If you work with babies, then you should look at the birth to 11 months and the 8-20 months spans. If you spend time with toddlers, then the 8-20 months and the 16-26 months are appropriate reminders. If you work with babies or toddlers whose development is already being slowed by disability or very limited early experience, then it is appropriate to look at a younger band. You can only identify appropriate next steps from a baby's or toddler's current point of development.

Some babies or toddlers may join your provision with their family already having a clear understanding, possibly a diagnosis, of how a disability is affecting their child's pattern of development. Usual good practice for partnership applies: you talk with parents to understand their child as an individual with familiar routines, likes and dislikes. Parents will be able to tell you about their baby or toddler's current ability level and any special help that will be needed. You are not expected to know everything about every disability. Good practice is to know how to find out more.

Parents will be experts about their own baby or toddler, but may not necessarily have had much help so far. They may also still be coming to terms with the consequences for their child and family of this disability or chronic health condition. In a group setting the SENCO should have more specialised knowledge and local contacts.

Personal, social and emotional development

It is complicated to explain and predict how young children manage some of their impressive developmental achievements. For instance, no single theory can fully explain how toddlers learn to speak a language within the very early years, with some toddlers learning more than one language. But the consistent messages about how adults – practitioners and parents – can best help do not point to complex techniques. The most positive experiences and opportunities for babies and toddlers are straightforward and a great deal rest upon treating them as individuals worthy of caring attention and personal interaction.

All the seven learning areas in the revised EYFS are important. However, as Moylett and Stewart (2012) explain, the three **prime** areas are more time-sensitive than the four **specific** areas of development. The earliest years of childhood are crucial for secure personal development, the building blocks for communication and healthy physical development. The great advantage of a Birth to Five years span, as established with the first EYFS framework, is that

it should demand respect for babies, toddlers and the youngest children as a whole. A huge amount happens before the third birthday and well-informed, emotionally warm adults make the difference at this crucial early time.

Social babies

If all is normal and going well, babies are born sociable. They are motivated to make physical and emotional contact with those adults who will become familiar. Babies use eye contact; sometimes a piercing and steady stare, and sound making; including crying, along with touch and a quite tight hold around manageable bits of the human body such as fingers or hair. Alert adults notice if young babies show few signs of being social, although in the early weeks and months it can be hard to assess what is wrong. Babies show a unique temperament from the earliest weeks, and some start and continue as more vocal and physically lively.

For babies and toddlers, the personal, social and emotional are all intertwined:

- They discover themselves, including the boundaries to their own body. But they need close physical contact and affectionate communication that gives them a sense of other people: their parents and a small number of other familiar adults, including their siblings.

- Their social life depends on the security of familiar routines, recognisable faces and ways of being handled. Even the most 'come-what-may' babies want some predictability in their life, so they can learn what is usual, and make sense of what is less usual or surprising.

- Their emotional life depends on feeling safe: that their physical needs will be met, that crying brings a familiar face and that familiar person will sooth their discomfort as well as make the most of their increasing wakefulness for chat and play.

Part of a close and personal relationship with babies and toddlers is that you are a welcome and playful companion: physically close, looking interested, responding and following the flow of the baby or young toddler's interests at that moment. Even good quality play resources for babies will never do the job on their own: how adults behave is the crucial component. The entire toy industry cannot come up with anything to replace a kindly, playful, familiar adult.

Human babies are equipped with some basic skills, which enable them to engage their familiar carers. The very young ones of our species cannot chase after us like little lambs. Babies cry for attention and, as hard as persistent crying can be on adult ears, it is a very effective message of 'I'm here and I want you now'. Babies are capable of a steady stare directed at the face of the person who holds them. As the weeks go by, the emergence of a small and then beaming smile, offers responses that are also key to holding the attention of other people–older siblings, as well as adult family members.

Babies pay close attention to their familiar carers. Yet they show a distinct interest in other babies and older children. It is important to be observant of this social development, since some books imply that under-twos are not interested in other children and their play. If you look closely, you will see many instances of babies who look at each other with an intent stare. They definitely look intrigued by babies as young as themselves, and they often have a steady stare at what another baby is doing.

The examples in this section come from recent observations of drop-in play sessions, but I have seen many similar exchanges in nurseries. The additional factor, when babies and toddlers come together on a regular basis, is that some of them certainly look like they recognise a familiar peer. Toddlers show recall of simple games that they played

together. They offer a toy or start a very simple repetitive game that they enjoyed earlier today or yesterday. It is definitely worthwhile thinking about how the adult organisation of a day, or of group provision, enhances or potentially restricts the social life of babies and toddlers.

Childminders usually have a mixed-age group sharing the same space – like the situation for many families.

LOOKING CLOSELY AT ONES

The babies (6-12 months of age) in the World of Discovery session (at The Flagship Centre) definitely looked interested in each other, during the time they spent together.

Jon (9 months) rolled confidently over onto all fours and looked intently at a sitting baby, close to him. He reached out and gently touched her foot. She in turn reached out equally gently and touched Jon's face.

Other babies in the session sometimes halted in their physical explorations in order to watch what another baby was doing. Sometimes they vocalised to each other; sometimes their varied sound making was aimed at the adults.

PARTNERSHIP WITH PARENTS: PLAY RESOURCES

Some bought play resources are very useful – the more open-ended materials that give plenty of scope for baby choice and exploration. However, some manufactured toys and related resources are a waste of space and money.

Some parents may be especially vulnerable to feeling that what they can buy – with all the inflated claims on some packaging – has to be better than what they can do in simple play with their baby or toddler. Conversation through the key person approach will be the way to guide learning at home in a considerate way. It is also crucial that you and your colleagues in group provision set a consistently good example in what you do with babies and toddlers.

We live in a technological age, but babies do not need, nor do they benefit from, an environment dominated by moulded plastic, battery-operated toys that are always noisy. Twenty-first century babies and toddlers are still keen on the potential of cardboard boxes, saucepans and wooden spoons.

The organisation of day nursery life has varied over the decades. By the mid-1970s, day nurseries had changed to mixed-age family grouping. Over the 1990s (approximately) there was a steady move back to age-banded rooms again. One practical issue seemed to be the different ratios required for best practice with babies and under-twos.

I have never encountered any research that studied ways of organising group provision and demonstrated a clear benefit to young children of one way over another. The most likely situation is that, like any early childhood experience, a very great deal depends on what familiar adults do and what they provide. From my own, informal observations of many settings, what seems to work best is an arrangement that enables babies and toddlers to have generous stretches of time with the slightly older children.

The very youngest children are fascinated by the older ones and what they do. There is a developmental advantage for the younger ones when they can potentially imitate play other than that of their age peers.

The slightly older children often show real pleasure in their time with the younger ones and relish the opportunity sometimes to have an apprentice in their play enterprises. Like in many families, the older children want times of

WHAT ARE CHILDREN LEARNING?

When you watch and listen to babies, it soon becomes clear that their personal and social development is closely intertwined with their physical skills and ability to communicate by sounds and movements.

Lucy (5 months) looked steadily at people's faces and her immediate environment. She had a broad smile and was engaged with me, an unfamiliar face, as well as with her mother, Louise.

Lucy loved peek-a-boo games. She enjoyed one when her nappy was changed and Louise got a cloth and hide her face. Lucy loved seeing Louise's face disappear and reappear. Lucy chortled, looked in anticipation and enjoyed several rounds of the game.

Lucy watched her older sister, Sophie, out in the garden. Lucy was keen to stare and liked looking at parts of the garden, when Louise walked around with her and held Lucy up to see clearly.

Lucy's liveliest times were with full-face contact with Louise, when Lucy was smiling, chortling and vocalising.

What have you noticed with babies you know well?

LOOKING CLOSELY AT ONES

I observed great interest between the babies and toddlers who were together in the Rumpus Drop-in.

Sue (14 months) looked at Marie (4½ months), who was feeding. Sue sat securely and played with one of the big tins. Alternating with looking at the babies, Sue was busy putting things in and taking them out again. Her greatest interest appeared to be in putting the tin lid in and out of the tin.

Sue and Jamie (6 months) spent time looking at each other. She looked at him and stretched out a hand. Sue was then holding a Teletubby™ which she stretched out and then gave to Jamie.

Sue was intrigued for a while in pushing the small toy that rotated and moved along the floor. Then she looked back at Marie again. Sue stretched out and touched Marie very gently, moved closer and touched her again.

Jamie was now playing with the lengths of chain, banging them on the black and white tin. Sue was also interested in the chain and pulling and exploring. She explored the wooden frame with red plastic in it. She enjoyed looking through it at her mother and giggled at this.

peace from younger ones, and reasonably object if their constructions and drawings are not protected from demolition by busy little hands.

A separate room or area for the very youngest children is not a closed space. Older children are welcome to visit the indoor area or the part of a garden that is especially for babies and toddlers. Mobile babies, and certainly walking toddlers, are able to choose to leave the indoor or outdoor space that is their home base. Low-level indoor or outdoor boundaries mean that older children can easily choose to 'chat' to the babies over the fence.

Warm personal relationships

Some babies and young toddlers will spend their first part of early childhood within their own family, although it is very unlikely that they will only spend time with their parents. Unless a family, or lone parent, is very isolated (a reason for possible concern and offering support), the social world of babies includes some time with their extended family and family friends. Some babies will start to spend some of their days with a childminder or an assigned key person in a nursery.

Babies can cope with more than one familiar adult: this pattern is normal family life for many of them. However, babies and toddlers cannot tolerate the stress of changes

if there are too many faces, bodies, smells and styles of care. So the key person approach is a non-negotiable part of early years practice and the revised EYFS statutory framework has confirmed this requirement. Childminders, and a named key person in nurseries, develop a close relationship with individual babies and their family. It is appropriate professional practice that babies, toddlers and young children form an emotionally warm and affectionate relationship with their key person and most likely another practitioner in a small group room.

Young children need to feel secure in the safety and comfort of your arms and lap. They need to be held and to hold in their turn. However, even babies need to feel the emotional foundation of having a secure place in your mind – your thoughts and feelings. They are never 'out of sight – out of mind'. You might like to think about how individual babies, for whom you are the key person or their childminder, feel that

LOOKING CLOSELY AT ONES

Some babies and toddlers will experience early years provision through a regular drop-in facility, where their parent or other family carer remains with them. Even with the continued presence of such a familiar figure, it is important that the atmosphere is peaceful and relaxed.

In the Rumpus drop-in, Marie (4½ months) was sitting on her mother's lap. Marie vocalised in a string of happy-sounding trills and then sucked her fingers. From the secure position on the lap, Marie looked in a steady gaze at Lesley (the drop-in leader).

Marie was also comfortable to be positioned, lying over her mother's bent leg. (Her mother was sitting on the floor.) Marie looked out and stretched out a hand. Her mother lifted up the cloth book that Marie was staring at. She was keen to look, touch and stare at the book.

Marie looked at her ease in different positions on the comfortable floor of the drop-in. She spent time on her stomach and then, a little later, lying on her back, Marie used a two-handed hold on a little tin, which caught her attention. She was able to bring it to her mouth.

Marie was interested in the solid wooden peg shapes, a bit like a mini skittle. She held one and dropped it, held and dropped again. Her mother moved Marie closer to a small resource that could be pushed around easily and had little coloured bits inside that were visible as it moved. Marie was able to push this backwards and forward and it spun around very easily. She was keen to touch and push it, then tried holding the side and was able to make it move in that way too.

PARTNERSHIP WITH PARENTS: RESPECT FOR FAMILY LIFE

Babies are born into a family that exists within an established social and cultural group. Some aspects of every family's life, which the key person needs to understand, will be influenced by the social and/or cultural traditions absorbed by this baby's parent(s).

All families live within a cultural context. It would be unreflective and poor practice, to behave as if families who share the practitioner's background run an 'ordinary' life, and anybody else is influenced by cultural differences.

Part of the role of the key person is to build a close, working relationship with the family of a baby or toddler. You need to understand parents' preferences as well as strongly held beliefs about baby care. You create the essential continuity between home and the baby's time with you. However, home life and your provision will not be identical in all aspects and babies can manage some minor differences between the style of familiar adults. It is professional to discuss any requests from parents that you are concerned might not be in the baby's best interests – whatever the apparent reason for that request.

Babies and toddlers are the ones who regard their daily life as 'ordinary'. It will be a long time before they notice and comment upon differences – some of which will highlight their own social and cultural identity. Those aspects of what make young children unique individuals will be part of a positive identity for young boys and girls, who have experienced care and affection and noticed the relationship of respect between the key person and their family.

you definitely have emotional and mental space for them, in your mind. In what ways do you show babies you are glad to see them, after a short gap, like the weekend? How do you make their personal care routines special for them? Do you fine-tune for baby and young toddler preference meaning it is never a one-size-fits-all for feeding or nappy changing?

A positive outlook on physical care and a nurturing environment are integral to the warm, personal relationship which must be the cornerstone of best early years practice with babies, toddlers and young children. Care – or nurture – and early learning are inseparable and any kind of early years provision has to be organised around that core understanding of what matters for young children's well-being.

If early years practitioners undervalue care and caring, that negative attitude undermines the quality of provision for three-

to five-year-olds. However, a disrespectful 'only care' outlook has really serious consequences for babies and toddlers, because they need demonstrably more caring support for their intimate physical needs. If the personal times of changing, feeding, resting, dressing and undressing are seen as 'wasted' time, then a significant proportion of every day with this very young age group will be wrongly dismissed as times when 'nothing important happens'.

Friendly, affectionate touch and easy physical contact is part of every day for babies and young toddlers. Babies show that they like to be close – not to any random adult, but with easy snuggling access to their familiar adults in the family and early years provision. Of course, babies – no more than toddlers or young children – should have cuddles foisted upon them, because the adult wants the contact. Considerate adults are easily available for babies and are sensitive to this baby's current mood and how they like, in general, to be touched and handled. This sensitivity creates a safe template for later interactions.

Adult choices over their behaviour make a big difference to the closeness of the relationship you develop with babies and very young children. However, what seems obvious to some practitioners, or perhaps to confident family members, as the right way to communicate and play with babies and very young toddlers, is not at all clear initially to less-experienced adults. For instance, many experienced practitioners have established the wise habit of being at the eye level of young children, whenever you are talking or listening to them. However, this behaviour is not 'just common sense', so that everyone acts in this way. Informal observation quickly shows that some practitioners and parents try to communicate with young children from their adult standing position, which often necessitates leaning over children.

Bending at the knees, or taking the tiny amount of extra time to sit beside a child, are learned ways of behaving. Inexperienced practitioners, or adults new to parenting, are guided by direct practical advice from a fellow adult who remains aware of what they now do, without having to think about it. Alternatively they learn from watching someone who behaves in this way and the reaction being so positive from the baby or child. Experienced early years practitioners need consciously to set a good example. Also, you are ready to advise less experienced colleagues, or offer suggestions to parents, along the lines of, "I find that ... makes a big difference to babies, because...".

Care and a nurturing environment

Babies' overall well-being is much more secure when practitioners value nurturing babies and young toddlers; within a social group that is small enough for these very young children to manage. The revised EYFS confirms that the key person approach is a non-negotiable part of early years practice in any kind of provision. The key person is responsible for ensuring an individual approach for care and learning within a continuing relationship with the baby or child and family. The revised statutory framework (pages 7 and 18, DfE 2012) is clear that this approach is not limited to a settling-in period.

The personal and emotional development of babies is supported when they have continuing experience of a familiar person, who – like their parents – has become more and more able to recognise this baby's moods and the different reasons that provoke these emotions.

- Quality early years practice ensures that babies receive prompt attention when they show signs of being hungry, thirsty or need their nappy changed.

- A supportive key person has learned, with the help of parents, how this baby shows tiredness and is ready for a daytime sleep.

- However, sensitive early years practitioners do not assume that fretfulness or complaining sounds are always signs that an older baby or toddler needs to be settled for sleep.

- Sometimes restlessness or physical fidgeting is a sign that this baby wants attention, movement, a trip out or something interesting to be shared with him or her.

- Babies are helped by friendly yet flexible routines and adult patience as they move slowly towards a daily routine that is closer to the pattern followed by slightly older children.

It is possible for the key person to take responsibility for most of the personal care of their key babies or toddlers. I have observed this pattern working smoothly in nurseries, where the team and the manager are committed to the emotional well-being of babies. This personal way of organising often goes hand-in-hand with the full recognition that babies and toddlers deserve the respect of a personal routine. They are changed when they need their nappy changed and not as part of an 'every baby gets changed' convenience schedule.

Childminders may seem to have a head start when it comes to opportunities for a family atmosphere. Yet, the best group provision has always rested on a homely physical environment and warm emotional atmosphere.

Babies and toddlers are individuals and they need small, intimate times. They do not 'do' groups. It is developmentally inappropriate to attempt anything larger than what I call a 'sofa-full'. It is a different matter if several babies or toddlers enthusiastically move across to get fully engaged in interesting resources, where there are already some children. Another possibility is that you find yourself surrounded by a number of bobbing young toddlers who have chosen to join what started as one adult dancing around with a baby in her or his arms.

These are spontaneous and physically active events, which have evolved because babies and toddlers made that choice. Some readers may have been given the advice or direction that they should plan group activities and expect babies and toddlers to join. I have encountered advice that circle time should be extended right to the babies, with the argument that this experience will help them in the transition to an older room, where this event will be part of a normal day.

I disagree with this advice – firstly on the developmental reasons outlined. Even if the plan is that babies experience singing, it is still much better practice to offer songs and rhymes in an informal and more intimate way, as and when babies would like this or toddlers indicate that they want a familiar song.

It is also important to challenge any approach to transition that rests upon importing practice with older children into a younger age range. Good practice with transition in group settings is the opposite approach: you establish continuity by taking what works well with the younger children into the next age-based room.

LOOKING CLOSELY AT ONES

In Southlands Crèche, the key person undertook the nappy changing and feeding for individual babies. However, the baby group was kept small: the responsibility of two practitioners who worked closely together. It was also striking that these practitioners were amongst the most experienced of a stable nursery team, in which many staff had years of commitment to children. The manager/owner of Southlands, like other excellent nurseries I have known, absolutely did not take the view that the baby room was the place to put the least experienced staff.

Toddlers, who had shown the awareness that they were ready for toilet training, were taken by their key person at regular times, attuned to this young child. There were end-of-day conversations between the key person and parent, as they shared the daily record and highlights of a baby or toddler's day.

In Grove House Infant and Toddler Centre, the key person also undertook their key babies' or toddlers' personal care. The centre had a built-in nappy changing area with an integral set of steps that could be pulled out. This facility meant that, once toddlers were steady on their feet, they could be active participants in this routine. Toddlers climbed up the steps and, with help, positioned themselves on the comfortable changing area. Everything necessary, including individual toiletry baskets, was stored within easy adult reaching distance.

Emotional expression

Babies and very young toddlers experience strong emotions, but they express themselves through actions and their body language. They are, as yet, unable to put those feelings into words.

You help them on this particular learning journey by offering empathy with very young children and accepting the emotions that they cannot, as yet, regulate in any way. You get to know them as individuals, so you are more able to make a good guess about how they probably feel. You use your own emotional vocabulary – words for feelings – long before you would expect a baby or young toddler to understand or use those words. You set the scene for learning, because your words, backed up by your body language, communicate 'you look happy, what a wonderful, big smile!' or 'you sound upset, what can I do to make things better?'.

Babies cry; it is their main form of communication in the early weeks and some cry a very great deal. It is crucial that early practitioners are not harsh on themselves with judgments like: 'Why can't I stop her crying?'.

In a group provision, there must be full team support for the key person to give time and comfort to a distraught baby. It is never spoiling to calm and cuddle a distressed baby or child. Touch, hold, rocking and cuddling will be a crucial part of reassuring the baby, as well as quiet talking or singing. You remain alert to what may be the main explanation for the crying. Sometimes there is a physical reason, but sometimes it is emotional. Occasionally, an older baby or young toddler is effectively crying out 'nothing personal, but I really don't want to be here'.

Sometimes you simply do not know why this baby continues to be harder to comfort than another of a similar age. If your relationship stretches into the future, then this 'cross' baby may grow into a firm toddler and two-year-old. At that point, she or he may find daily life much more straightforward, now that preferences and objections can be expressed in spoken words. Your patience in the baby months, and that of the baby's family, will pay off now. Fretful babies, whose key adults have been unable or willing to comfort through the crying, seem very likely to continue as annoyed toddlers.

It is developmentally inappropriate – and therefore unprofessional for early years practitioners – to label babies or toddlers as 'clingy' or to treat that pattern of behaviour as a 'problem' to be 'managed' out of existence. It is very normal that this age group wants to be close to a familiar adult – that is why you will sometimes be in a cuddle-huddle with several babies or toddlers.

Babies and toddlers will head away from you, their key person, when they feel secure. They will hold tight or want

WHAT ARE CHILDREN LEARNING?

Mobile babies and physically active toddlers will 'get into everything'; it comes with the job description of being such a very young child. They will use their physical skills to the best of their ability and sometimes with great vigour. Your encouragement of active babies needs to co-exist with friendly guidance that respects their personal world and their limited social understanding.

Babies and toddlers do not know which items are for play and which should not be poked, shaken or dropped. In a family home, there may be more non-play items of great interest than in a nursery, which is a specially designed environment. However, this issue can arise in nurseries, at the very least that human play companions can be hurt in ways that teddies cannot.

Gentle, and sometimes firm, guidance is needed to tell older babies and toddlers that it is not alright to pull your hair or poke you with a sharp little finger. Your appropriate use of the word 'no' and matching facial expression starts the process of guiding very young children, who cannot yet be expected to guide themselves. 'No' is only a troublesome word if it is used frequently by tetchy adults, who do not explain simply why this action is not alright.

to be very close when they do not feel okay, or are uncertain for some reason. They will show you when they are comfortable to extend the invisible elastic and move away, although they may well check on you by looking.

It is inevitable within shared care that the adults – parents and practitioners – need to ease the handover at the beginning and end of the day.

● You help a baby or toddler with the daily separation from their parent when you are ready to reassure, cuddle and talk gently. The baby, as well as parent, needs to feel that there is an unrushed transfer from one safe pair of hands over to another.

● A key person should have become familiar with this baby or young toddler. You have learned that this young child

LOOKING CLOSELY AT ONES

In Grove House Infant and Toddler Centre the practitioners remained close to the babies and toddlers, so they were able easily to support very young social interaction and help out, if necessary.

Babies and toddlers often showed obvious interest in each other. Indoors there was always a practitioner sitting close, often on the floor, so it was straightforward to offer gentle guidance, if baby or toddler attempts to make contact were a bit too vigorous for their peer. I observed more than once how a calm practitioner helped a toddler or very young two to say to another, "I don't like it. Don't." These still very young children were being supported as they started to deal with situations themselves.

Like any normal day with very young children, the practitioners themselves were sometimes on the receiving end of friendly toddler pats that became increasingly forceful. Again, older babies or toddlers were guided by words and a facial expression that communicated 'that's not how we treat friends'.

Babies and young toddlers do not understand the concept of 'sharing' and they are not able to wait for 'their turn'. The Grove House team had created, and continued to develop, a learning environment with a generous supply of open-ended play resources. These were organised in labelled baskets, which older babies and toddlers were able to pull out for themselves.

Practitioners were sitting on the floor with the children, so it was easy for an adult to ensure that resources were within easy reach and discretely move some across to a baby who had only a limited supply.

is reassured by staring together at a particular picture or going into the garden. Your response is based on your knowledge and personal relationship.

A learning journey towards self regulation

Babies and toddlers are at the very beginning of a learning journey to establish habits of positive, prosocial behaviour and to learn to exercise some self control. Babies have neither the understanding, nor the plotting power, to be held accountable for the consequences of their actions. Friendly adults deal with these practical issues within the physical environment created for babies and toddlers and in your support for baby play within a social atmosphere. Babies and young toddlers make moves towards each other and regular social contact creates the happy recognition that is the basis for very young friendships. Babies lean out to touch each other and sometimes engage in whole body hugs, which can tip over both individuals. You keep a watch, but avoid over-reacting, because this friendly wrestling does not necessarily hurt. Sometimes you just need to help two rather surprised older babies back into the upright position.

You need to be alert to little fingers in eyes or ears, and hands in hair. But these social moves are not only between baby peers. Older siblings or non-related children, who have

responded well to requests to be careful with the baby, are sometimes themselves on the receiving end of serious baby poking and toddler pinching. They need to be enabled to escape, especially if they are in a fixed position, such as sharing a double buggy.

Older babies start to understand 'no' and there are occasions when this word, backed up with gentle physical guidance, is appropriate. New little teeth can be sharp and, although babies do not intend to hurt, it is wise to guide them to chew on safe items and not someone's finger.

You can guide older babies and toddlers towards kindly behaviour but you need to keep your adult language very simple indeed. Recall that babies and very young children are physical; they do not have the understanding to be 'aggressive'.

However, physically rough strategies – perhaps to secure a toy they want – need to be converted, with your direct guidance, towards other options. You move in calmly, ideally before babies or toddlers have become tearful and ensure that everyone is safe. You acknowledge with words that "you both want the teddy" and, depending on your knowledge of these individuals, you may gather both babies and the teddy into your lap. You may discretely pull in another soft toy that you guess could be equally attractive.

The ways in which babies and toddlers play are partly shaped by their level of development: their physical skills, ability to communicate and social awareness of others. Yet, thoughtful adults make a significant difference to the learning environment in which babies and toddlers spend their days.

In a welcoming environment, babies and toddlers show that they are at ease by their behaviour. Very young children settle into the flow of a homely nursery or the actual home of their childminder. However, regular attendance at a drop-in can enable toddlers to look very much at home when the environment and routines have been carefully considered by the leader and team.

The early years practitioners, in settings I visited for this book, had thought carefully about play resources. They had created an environment in which life was easier for babies and they continued to be alert to how babies and toddlers experienced resources and appropriate activities. These babies and toddlers did not have to tolerate levels of waiting or turn-taking, which were developmentally beyond their capability.

When toddlers were outdoors, there could be practical issues if several children wanted the same wheeled vehicle. However, practitioners were often able to negotiate simple deals with toddlers. These very young children were far more open to compromise than if their whole day had been full of turn-taking issues.

WHAT ARE CHILDREN LEARNING?

You reach supported conclusions about the personal well being of a very young child by watching how they behave. They will not yet tell you in words how they feel.

Look at this example of Steven and consider what this description tells you, not only about his personal development, but also his skills in other areas of learning.

In the Rumpus Drop-in I watched Steven (19 months), who was confident with his walking and moving about the well-resourced room.

He was able to stand securely, bend at the waist from standing and then come upright again – all very steady.

But Steven also showed toddler confidence as he organised his own chosen play from the play resources.

Steven was engaged in sustained play with a zig-zag wooden ramp on which a small wheeled vehicle can roll down. He was able to put his little wooden train on the narrow ramp, watch it run down, then pick it up and put it back again.

Steven was also confident walking around carrying one of the vehicles to somewhere else he wished to be, sit down on a cushion, still holding the train. He also walked across the room to show his train to an adult and back again. He then returned across the room, pausing to experiment with balancing the train on his head, with some success.

Steven then took the train and tried it on the laid out wooden railway. He placed the vehicle very carefully and got it to work on the track. Steven managed to get the train to go through the tunnel part way. Then he faced a problem because he could not stretch to push the train all the way from the end where he was. He was successful by working it out from the other end.

Steven was then sitting in the middle of the laid-out tracks and putting his train back on the track and very carefully manoeuvring it along.

At 19 months, Steven was able to look carefully to place this wooden train on the zig-zag ramp and also on the wooden railway tracks.

Rebecca (3yrs, 3 mths) was also playing with the wooden track. At one point, the two children's trains came head to head. Steven made protesting noises but was unsure what to do. Then Rebecca resolved the impasse by offering to Steven, "You go first", which he did.

Communication and language

Happy exchanges during the earliest part of childhood, lay firm foundations for older toddlers and then twos, to be keen to talk and express their ideas. Young children's ability to listen starts with experiencing respect from familiar adults who show they want to listen to, and enjoy joint looking with, babies and young toddlers.

The building blocks for the turn-taking of genuine conversation can be established long before the child, in this communicative exchange, has any recognisable words.

Daily life and support for communication

There can be a significant gap in the size of children's working vocabulary between those who have had a good start in communication and those children who have been poorly served by their early experiences.

- The desire to communicate and the steady building of vocabulary are well supported by natural, daily exchanges that arise through shared play and joint experiences.

- Helpful adults do not sit down to plan structured 'communication activities' – not with any young children and certainly not with babies or toddlers.

- Communication is personal and flows from what interests this baby, toddler or child, today.

   - Simple works. What really matters is that adults listen to, talk with, interact and play with babies and young children.

- The support from a planning adult's outlook is that opportunities and experiences are offered (not imposed) which, from practitioners' knowledge of individual babies and toddlers, are likely to interest and excite them.

● Young children do not need special language programmes and remedial help when their early years have been full of personal, attentive communication – at home but also in their early years provision.

● On the other hand, special help will be needed if it becomes clear that sensory or other disabilities are affecting how this baby's communication can develop.

It is appropriate to encourage a heightened awareness in the early years workforce of the difficulties encountered by vulnerable families. However, this focus must not build an inaccurate problematic image for families in general. Alertness to the importance of early intervention has to co-exist with the recognition that, in terms of development and family life, many babies and toddlers are absolutely fine and their family life is happy. The enhanced focus in the revised EYFS about active promotion of learning at home has to rest upon respect from practitioners. Many parents are already doing a great deal to support the development of their baby or toddler.

Researchers who study communication and language use terms with very specific meanings, as well as making a very detailed analysis of how language and different world languages are structured. In research, the term 'speech' refers to sound patterns of a given world language and 'language' refers to the structure and meaning of a given language. It is valuable to understand this distinction, especially when you read about studies of linguistic development. However, in daily practice with young children, the word 'language' tends to be used to cover both these aspects.

The task for very young children learning their family language(s) is to become familiar with the sound patterns of a language. Babies are very sensitive to the sound patterns of language that they hear. This sensitivity starts before they are born, when they can hear sounds from outside the womb – most clearly the voice of their mother. Long before babies can say actual words, they are very alert to the sound patterns of their family language(s). They pay close attention to the faces and mouths of their parents and other familiar carers.

Babies' communicative utterances over the first year of life include language-like sounds and strings of sound. By the end of their baby year, those sounds are becoming much closer to the sound patterns of their family language(s). What you hear from babies is the observable part of what is happening in their brain. Babies are born ready to learn any language. Then, over their first twelve months, their brain becomes more specialised for the language(s) they hear. By one year of age, babies can no longer discriminate subtle differences in sounds that are unnecessary for their home language(s).

In spoken language and different versions of the same language, you will hear the way in which a word is spoken. In a word with more than one syllable, does the emphasis fall on one syllable more than another? Some languages, like English, are spoken with a distinctly greater stress on one syllable more than another. For instance, 'dinner' is said with more stress on 'din' than 'ner' – try saying it the other way around. English is a language with audible differences in syllable stress. In contrast, French or Spanish is spoken with equal stress placed on each syllable. Babies and toddlers are also gaining experience in this subtle aspect to language.

WHAT ARE CHILDREN LEARNING?

Children need good reasons – from their point of view – to want to talk and to listen. They need plenty of early experiences of familiar adults who listen to them. Positive relationships – part of their personal, social and emotional development, are an integral part of growing skills of communication.

It is normal life for toddlers and young children that they struggle with the search for words and tolerate the frustration of making other people understand. Very young girls and boys will persevere in this task, when they are confident familiar adults genuinely chatting. Young toddlers also forgive those times when a familiar adult seems to be very dense: failing to understand what is obvious to the gesticulating toddler.

Look closely at babies who are in your care.

Encourage parents to appreciate all the little signs of individual early communication.

Here are some highlights from the first year of my daughter, Tanith.

- Tanith was a rather serious baby and frowned quite a lot. Some babies are smiling from 4-6 weeks old. Tanith was 7-weeks-old before I got a definite grin from her.

- By 8 weeks she had a range of coo-ing sounds and soft aahs, as well as a strong cry. What appeared to be deliberate gurgling noises soon followed.

- Over her third month, Tanith's ability to stare at people's faces seemed to be a strategy to communicate. Her face lit up at a response.

  - She then usually made a stream of sounds, kicked her legs and moved her arms about in a lively fashion.

- In her fourth month, Tanith held sustained 'conversations' with us and sometimes laughed with her mouth wide open.

  - Her sound making and turn-taking in communication extended over the following weeks.

- By 7 months Tanith's communication included double-syllable sounds and long strings of sound in a sustained flow. She also leaned towards us as she 'spoke'.

- By her ninth month, she turned in a reliable way to her name, said by us or her older brother: Drew liked to get his baby sister's personal attention in this way.

- Tanith liked to have Drew play with her, and rewarded him with big smiles. One of her favourites was what Drew called 'playing nose': a game of touching nose-to-nose.

- Towards the end of her baby year, Tanith's own utterances were very chatty and had conversational expression and pacing.

  - She participated in a turn-taking conversation, although without recognisable words from her.

Babies as active communicators

Observant parents and early years practitioners have always commented on the alertness of babies and how much happens before the first recognisable words.

- With personal attention, young babies are active partners in the very early communicative exchanges within the family. They imitate the expression of a their parent, or other carer, but do not only copy. They are active in their own facial expressions and communicate their feelings with waving hands and feet, within their current physical skills.

- Once babies have reached only three or four months of age, you will notice that they make sounds, but that they also pause and look expectant.

- With the experience of regular, friendly attention since birth, young babies have already learned something of the timing of a conversation.

- Unless they have disabilities that affect sight or hearing, babies react to small changes in the tone of voice or facial expression of a familiar adult.

- They are also sensitive to when your attention is distracted, perhaps by another adult or child talking with you.

● Babies who are already confident about communicating, often make physical movements and vigorous sounds, which definitely look like attempts to regain your full attention.

● Sadly, babies who have not experienced much attention, or it has been very unpredictable, will give up trying – sooner or later.

Older babies become very chatty because they have had generous personal attention over their baby year. They are able to use gesture to indicate what is of current interest to them.

Older babies now have more control over their hands and arms. They are able to look at something intently, point with their eyes, then point with a finger or whole hand. Any genuine conversation needs a shared focus on what is in front of both of you. So you follow the gaze of babies and young toddlers, listen to what they 'say' and add your own simple comments.

You become familiar with the combination of gestures and overall body language that this baby or toddler uses to communicate messages: 'I'm pleased to see you', 'where's that gone?', 'I'm not sure about this' and 'will you stop me again?'. The best communication with babies and toddlers picks up on these messages as you gaze and touch in your turn. Your words add the accompanying message of, 'and hello to you too!', 'let's have a look together' or 'you didn't like that?'.

You need to be comfortable, from the early baby months, to gesture appropriately, as well as talk with babies.

● It often feels natural to adults to make a drinking movement or put fingers to mouth when they are asking: "Would you like a drink?" or "Are you hungry?".

● Be ready to use pointing and touch to: track a moving object, direct a baby's attention or emphasise a game or song, such as touching toes as part of "Where are your toes?".

● Pointing used with words is a practical way to help babies and then toddlers to make sense of naming words, such as: "There's your rabbit" or finding something in a page of a favourite book.

Notice how older babies and toddlers use regular gestures to accompany their meaningful sounds and the early words, and that they do not stop gesturing once the recognisable words emerge. Your generous use of gesture and pointing is also a help to very young children whose home language is not that of their nursery or childminder.

An emotionally warm atmosphere

In the world of babies and toddlers, all areas of learning intermingle to form their whole life experience. It is very noticeable how much their personal, social and emotional development interacts with the development of communication skills. Babies will not flourish in an atmosphere full of stress and rush. They need time and a friendly sense of timing to their days. Their emotional environment is just as important as their physical surroundings.

In a relaxed family home or group provision, familiar adults are fully alert to gesture: their own and that of the babies. Experienced early years practitioners know that body language is a crucial part of communication – and it does not stop with the end of the toddler year. In an emotionally warm atmosphere, babies will let you know what they want, think and feel, or what the problem is from their perspective. The adult problem is often to be the 'detective' and work out what is not immediately obvious. Close relationships, and the key person approach in group settings, are so important because it is the only way you get to recognise what a baby or young toddler is telling you by their actions.

Uncommunicative babies?

It is usual that babies imitate actions and sounds that are within their capabilities. So it should concern you if a baby or young toddler is unresponsive to the actions of familiar others. In a similar way it should catch your attention if older babies and young toddlers do not show that they have a growing understanding of their own personal world. People and places should have become familiar. It is realistic to expect that young toddlers know what to do with common items for their play or domestic routines.

You should be concerned over young babies who do not make sounds or respond around 3-4 months to the give-and-take of adult words and baby sound making. In the normal course of events, babies are socially responsive, they show awareness of their immediate surroundings, an interest in human faces and an alertness to the sounds of human speech. As the months pass, you should be concerned if older babies do not eye-point or then finger point to people and items that interest them.

Over the first year of life you should notice an increased enthusiasm for sound-making and for social interaction. Familiar adults – parents and practitioners – need to be alert for babies who do not react or seem socially uninterested. It can be hard to assess sight and hearing for babies, especially if the loss is partial. However, familiar carers are often the first people to realise that this baby does not react to what you say, unless she or he can see you too.

Sometimes it becomes clear within the first or second year of life that some kind of disability is affecting the development of communication for this baby or toddler. However, some uncommunicative babies have given up trying, because of their very limited early experiences. Familiar adults have to give time and attention. Vulnerable babies or toddlers may

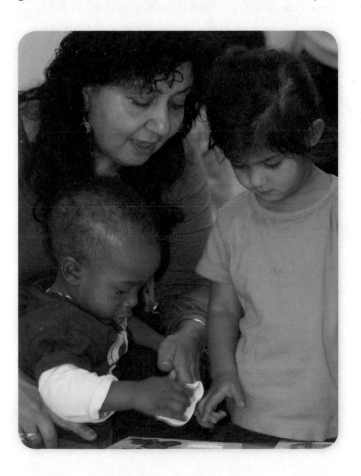

In Southlands Crèche, a great deal of thought and planning has gone into creating a relaxed day for the babies and very young toddlers in the small groups that make up this provision. Josie and Cindy, who run the baby room team, go out in the local neighbourhood every day. Time spent indoors is unhurried and takes account of the different personal routines of individual babies. Within the flow of the day there is still generous time for these babies and young toddlers to explore a wide range of open-ended materials.

I observed many occasions when mobile babies and very young toddlers were able to drive their own learning through the resources they chose. There was sometimes a great deal of friendly communication, without many actual words spoken.

- During one afternoon, Tammy, a very young toddler, was obviously enjoying a book, comfortable and snuggled up to Josie. Tammy looked closely at the book and already understood how to turn the pages. She was also able and keen to put the book back into the container (a low wooden open storage system) and choose another book by herself.

- Charlie (14 months) was made welcome to join with the impromptu storytime with Josie and Tammy. But he was busy exploring the large collection of plastic bottles. Something different had been placed in each bottle and the top made secure. Charlie selected bottles in a deliberate way and one at a time.

- He experimented with what they would do and discovered that some bottles made a sound, sometimes a rattle. Charlie repeated his actions, looking and listening carefully. The contents of some bottles moved around more than others and a vigorous shaking brought about much shifting of the materials inside.

- A low mirror in the room enabled babies and toddlers to look at themselves and others in reflection. For some time Charlie intently watched himself in the process of shaking different bottles.

- Despite his concentration on exploring the bottles, Charlie continued to be aware of the adults in the room. More than once, he looked across to Josie, who was able to smile her interest and that she definitely had kept Charlie in mind. I had become a familiar face in the room and at one point Charlie looked at me and smiled, as I watched him try different ways of making sounds.

PARTNERSHIP WITH PARENTS: CHAT WITH BABIES

Parents and other family carers need to see your good example of how to communicate with babies long before they have any words. Perhaps you can also share these important pointers in a family workshop or to support less-experienced colleagues.

- Be close to an individual baby so that your faces are in close proximity. Babies need to see your eyes and facial expression.

- You can chat in this way as you change their nappy, hold them secure on your lap or sit beside babies as they lay on their back on a comfortable floor.

- It does not matter what you say, so long as you look interested. Use ordinary words, keeping what you say simple and your phrases short.

- Pause and look expectant, so that babies learn it is now their turn to 'say' something.

- Be more expressive than usual speech, both in how you say the words and in your facial expression.

- Babies like voices to be slightly higher pitched than normal adult tone. They enjoy a slightly sing-song style, with a circling and repetitive quality.

- Repeat a phrase that has caught the baby's attention, such as: "Is that a raspberry? Did you blow a raspberry at me?".

- Give babies time to express their sounds, make their facial expression or wave their hands at you. Too fast and you talk over the baby's contribution.

- Sometimes follow the baby's lead, in sounds or facial expression. They are delighted when you imitate them.

live in families where the adults are overwhelmed by their other problems. Family support is needed also when the primary carer of a baby is depressed.

A different problem can arise for parents who want to do their best, yet are misled by the aggressive marketing of technological play resources aimed at babies. Some promotional material strongly implies that bought items will teach children to speak. However, the entire toy and DVD industry cannot come up with anything that beats a communicative, affectionate real adult for fostering vital, early skills of communication.

Additionally, laptops or DVDs marketed to parents of babies sometimes claim that the product will promote learning of colour or number. This claim is developmental nonsense: babies have not yet worked out the symbolic nature of language applied to familiar objects and people. Abstract concepts like colour only make sense later, following plenty of hands-on, eyes-on, first-hand experiences.

Adult language in context

Babies and toddlers – and children in general – need first-hand experiences. They need a rich array of open-ended resources and plenty of scope to determine for themselves the direction of an activity that interests them. If practitioners are tempted to pre-package and over-organise experiences, there is far less potential for babies or children to be active themselves and to extend their current understanding of the world.

Babies' and toddlers' motivation to express themselves rests partly on their growing knowledge of their world, and the ways in which familiar adults have used their spoken language to comment, meaningfully, within play experiences. Any play resource needs to have generous possibilities and that it can be used in different ways, combined with other items. The serious problem with some commercially produced toys is that the possibilities have already been severely limited. The moulded 'early learning' table or stand cannot be taken apart. There is no point in making sounds to and on behalf of some dolls or teddies, because a push on their stomach releases a stream of pre-recorded comments. Open-ended play resources, and an alert, playful, adult companion are an excellent combination. Your skills of communication and your brain are also engaged in a natural conversational flow, because you can never predict how individual babies will use open-ended materials.

Long before babies or toddlers will use the words themselves, they need to hear familiar adults comment in a meaningful way on what is happening right now. Words link to an event, a play resource or an action. Adults' conversation and brief commentary makes sense because they have followed the immediate interest of a baby or toddler. In all of the examples in this section, the one or two adults closely involved in the experience watched what individual babies or toddlers chose to do with the materials. The adult was sitting right by the babies or toddlers, at their physical level. So she (in these examples the practitioners were female) was able to comment briefly, but to the point, about what the baby did. The adult comments were also sometimes about what the adult herself was doing with her own pile of materials.

Supporting toddlers' speech

Toddlers vary in their development, but over the second year of life you should hear recognisable words emerging. You would not expect chatty toddlers to be easily understood

LOOKING CLOSELY AT ONES

In the toddlers' group room of Buckingham's Nursery, I watched a happy sequence in which two very young children sat with one adult and took their time in exploring their own little pile of fresh sticky strawberry rice mix, which was ladled onto the table in front of the children.

The toddlers put their hands in their rice, poked it and squeezed. The adult also had her own pile, so toddlers sometimes watched what she was doing. When one pair of toddlers showed that they were ready to stop, the practitioner invited them to help with clearing up their rice. Then they went together to the bathroom to wash their hands. With no sense of rush, another two toddlers were then asked if they would like to try the strawberry rice.

The practitioner sitting with the toddlers made brief comments about the feel and look of the rice. So toddlers were able to connect her words, "it's sticky", with the texture they could touch and the smell, "it's strawberry rice" with the fragrance that had been mixed into the rice. She watched what each toddler chose to do with their own rice commenting that their hand was "sticky" too.

Meaningful connections for the toddlers continued into the hand-wiping phase, since the practitioner took the natural opportunity to say, "It's dark in here" before she switched on the light in the bathroom. These connections continued when one of the toddlers, now all cleaned up and no longer sticky, joined another adult on the other side of the room. This adult commented with a friendly tone of voice: "What do you smell of?". She then smelled the toddler's hand and asked: "Do you smell of strawberries?".

LOOKING CLOSELY AT ONES

I observed many instances in Buckingham's Nursery of hands-on sensory experiences for babies. One morning, three babies (in a suitable child seat at a low table) happily patted their hands into their own personal little pile of jelly.

On another day, three or four babies crawled into or sat directly in a store of sand spread by an adult across a large tuff-spot. The babies could get their hands into the sand, wriggle bare toes in it and still be safe, since an adult was also sitting in the sand and gently stopped the one baby who was keen to put sand in her mouth.

A sitting baby concentrated for close to 15 minutes exploring his personal, favourite resource: a low basket with a generous collection of ribbons and some sparkly material. He was keen to hold and pull, look and touch. Soon this baby had most of the ribbons out of the basket and spread over his lap.

I watched as one baby was held in an adult's arms for him to grasp the ribbons that dangled from a secure fixed point in the ceiling. A second baby, sitting on the floor, eye-pointed that he was interested too and straightaway he was offered "do you want the ribbons?" and lifted up so he could grasp and bat the ribbons about.

by an unfamiliar adult. But they will be largely understood – words and all their back-up gestures – by familiar adults and often also by siblings or familiar older children in the same early years provision.

Toddlers' spoken vocabulary extends because they hear a wide range of words used in a meaningful context and the toddler, or very young child, is comfortable to repeat back the word or phrase out of choice, producing an almost echo. The first words of toddlers relate to familiar people, animals or objects in this individual's daily life. So, there is no definitive 'first 20 words'; every toddler's life is different. Some highlights overleaf are from the diary I kept of my daughter, Tanith. What examples do you have of toddlers you know very well?

It cannot be stressed enough that communication with babies and young children is between individuals – a familiar adult and very few children. It is developmentally unwise practice to

try to do group communication with babies and toddlers (or any under-threes).

When you are close, it is easy to ensure you have the attention of a baby or toddler before you start: use gentle touch, eye contact and a smile or the baby's name. Pause and then say something, or point out something of interest. Sometimes, the communication starts because this baby or young toddler has engaged your attention. It is important to relax, and to avoid taking over the talk. You need to trust what I call the power of the pause: that vital gap when the baby or young toddler is thinking and gathering their sounds and basic words.

You may sometimes repeat what a toddler says and extend a little by adding a relevant comment. For instance, an older baby or young toddler directs your attention to the big sunflowers, swaying the breeze. Perhaps she or he tries their personal word that is close to 'flower'. You respond with something like: "Yes, look at our sunflowers" then pause and add "see them move from side to side" and use a gesture that mimics the swaying of the flowers.

You say any words correctly as you reply – so a word-sound like 'fower' is reflected back as 'flower' with the sound blend that this toddler cannot yet manage. You do not make the toddler repeat the correct version, because this kind of pressure can be disheartening. In a relaxed atmosphere, you will often hear a toddler echo what you have said; they do their own practice out of choice.

Your communication with babies and toddlers needs to be adjusted to their personal temperament and their current mood. Helpful adults are not all-singing-all-dancing every moment of the day, or even over the whole session lasting a couple of hours. You, and the baby or toddler, would be exhausted. But also good communication has quieter moments: the light and shade of personal exchanges.

You will then observe how a toddler's working vocabulary grows over the second year of life. Again, I have summarised some highlights from my daughter's toddler year. What have you, and a toddler's own parents, noticed in their individual version of early language?

Two or more languages

Some babies and toddlers become aware of two (or occasionally more) languages over their first or second year of life. It is ideal if their childminder or key person in nursery is fluent in the baby or toddler's home language. But frequently – given the wide diversity of languages now in the UK – this pairing will not be an option.

- However, even a bilingual practitioner needs to support a toddler to build vocabulary in English, the common

LOOKING CLOSELY AT ONES

By 14 months Tanith made deliberate sounds that worked as words. She said 'ca' – first to the family pet and then to other cats in the neighbourhood. Tanith said 'hello' or 'hiya' in context and she used 'Mama' and 'Dada' to us. She said 'bubbles' – reflecting her daily experience of a lot of blowing bubbles, playing with foamy water and baby bubble bath at night.

Tanith had the useful words of 'more' and 'no' and was taught to say 'Ta' by her three-year-old brother Drew, who was very pleased with this achievement.

At this age Tanith tried hard to imitate many more words, which bit-by-bit then entered her spontaneous language.

Tanith showed that she understood more words in context. She understood 'no', even if she was disinclined sometimes to follow it. She responded clearly to: "Do you want a..?" followed by other familiar words such as 'a drink'.

She could follow simple requests such as: "Get your shoes" and was happy to take items 'to Drew' or 'to Daddy'.

shared language across the UK. If you do not make this steady shift, then later this baby or toddler will not be able to talk with their two- or three-year-old peers.

● If you have no experience of this family language, then it is best practice and good partnership with parents, to learn some key phrases that will be of practical use.

● Do not limit your communication with a baby or toddler to a family language in which you have a very limited vocabulary. You will restrict what the child can talk about and understand from you.

LOOKING CLOSELY AT ONES

Tanith's first recognisable words arose from authentic experiences within her daily life and her familiar routines.

● By 18 months she used words for familiar items: shoe, stick, car, mil(k), chee(se), ca(t), train (which came out more like 'dee'), dog, sock, gop (her vitamin drops), coco (pops), chip, bin, bag, key and book.

● She also had a range of useful words that would operate as requests, descriptions or suggestions: 'all gone', 'no more', 'down', 'up', 'go' and 'look'.

● Some words made no sense unless you were familiar with Tanith's personal world. For instance, we are a household that plays a lot of music. Tanith's most frequent toddler requests were 'ga-ga', meaning Radio Ga Ga by Queen and 'rock' for Fraggle Rock, the theme from a popular children's programme.

● She also used animal sounds in context – 'miaow' and 'woof-woof', and a growling sound for monsters.

● It was noticeable over this time that Tanith made even greater efforts to copy words that she heard. She was keen to join in her favourite songs or rhymes, and was able to request some by the opening words or repeated phrase.

● By 18-19 months Tanith had started to combine words; 'more juice', specifying 'apple juice' or 'orange juice' as a choice and 'Drew bang'. She also copied some of Drew's favourite phrases, in particular 'I know that!'.

From this base, Tanith steadily added words to her working vocabulary, with a significant increase over the period when she was 20-22 months. So by 23 months the list I had was of over 150 words, of different kinds, along with short phrases of two or three words.

● Ask parents to help you with tapes of songs or rhymes in their home language – or ensure that you learn a song thoroughly because this mother or father is happy to join you a few times in singing with the children.

● As with any young child, you need to find out about a young toddler's personal words, for important routines like meals, naps or nappy changing.

The same principles of effective communication apply for toddlers on the road to becoming bilingual as for monolingual children. You talk simply about what is front of both of you and the immediate experience – either in terms of this personal care routine or the open-ended resources that you are both enjoying at the moment.

Communication and a baby's world

Babies' skills of communication develop within their social world: their own community of important other people. Conversations – long before babies have actual words – happen within routines, events and local outings that extend their understanding of the broader world, just as much as their powers of communication.

Babies and young toddlers experience a sense of community through their immediate environment. When you share the care of young children, part of your responsibility is to understand

LOOKING CLOSELY AT ONES

In the Southlands Crèche, the baby room team are committed to get out every day with the babies into the neighbourhood. It has to be seriously unwelcome weather to stop them.

Sometimes they make the walk into the nearby town centre. The babies and young toddlers experience interesting events of ordinary life such as buying vegetables from the market. They regularly get out to the local park, enjoying a picnic in warmer weather. There is relaxed time to look at the flowers, watch the birds and listen to the sounds of the outdoors.

Of course, babies and very young toddlers sometimes fall asleep in their buggy – that is a normal event – and some restless babies are very soothed by the movement of travelling along, as well as friendly chat to them.

The crèche has been located here for some time and the staff group is stable. Consequently, they have come to know many people who live locally. Part of a normal outing is that they stop and chat with, or are greeted by, familiar adults. The babies and toddlers experience that they too are part of this local community.

who and what is significant in this baby or toddler's personal and social world. You cannot have meaningful conversations, nor understand toddlers' early words and phrases, if you are utterly puzzled about their world beyond their time with you. Who is in their family, immediate and extended? Who has become familiar to them, including while they are in your care? This question includes other babies and children as well as important adults like their key person.

Time for babies is very much about personal timing and happy routines within the shape of a day. Over the baby year and into the toddler months, they begin to understand and welcome the familiarity of routines, so long as the adult choices about timing support intimate physical care and babies do not feel rushed or harassed. Young babies start to recognise the sounds, smells or adult preparations that mean that mealtime or bath time is about to start. The timing and sequence of a nappy change should be a personal experience and a time of warm communication. So, long before clock time, days or seasons have any meaning at all, babies get a feel for 'what happens here' and 'what that means for me'.

Until mobile toddlers can walk at least short distance on an outing, then babies will travel from place to place in a buggy, unless they are strapped or wrapped to your body. Babies need to feel fully engaged in the experience of going out and about. Buggies are a fine invention, but it is important that the equipment does not end up creating an emotional distance between the baby and the adult.

Suzanne Zeedyk (2008) carried out research into how adults communicate with babies, depending on the style of buggy that was used. She looked at babies and toddlers (under-twos) and found that parents tended to talk more to the infants when they were sat in a buggy that faced the adult (what the research called the toward-facing style of buggy). The study raised important issues about what may encourage adults – practitioners as well as the parents in Zeedyk's study – to chat with babies and very young children as a normal part of the daily routine. The practical implications of research about buggies need to be taken with care.

- Wheeled equipment does not work communication magic. Experiences for babies depend on what people do – the equipment with the legs and voice. A towards-facing buggy cannot itself be more emotionally healthy for the baby.

- Many adults talk on their mobile phone while pushing a toward-facing buggy. Those babies learn that they are far less important than the magic box in the adult's hand. These toddlers learn that they are insignificant compared with whoever is on the other end.

- The key issue is that communication is part of this outing. If babies are in a towards-facing buggy, then you can chat with them on the trip, whilst being alert to where you are going.

- If you have outward-facing buggies, then you need to stop regularly, get to the baby or toddler's level, look together and chat. A towards-facing buggy will have to be turned on occasion, so older babies can look in the same direction as you.

- The buggy style to avoid has to be the two-level double buggy, in which one baby or child is tucked away in the lower section, with few options of talking with anyone, or seeing what is happening around them.

An understanding of personal time and place is also supported by regular, frequent experiences of going out and about in the local community. Babies and young toddlers can get to know a familiar neighbourhood, start to recognise the last corner before you reach the market and get excited because part of this outing is that you always buy some fruit from this stall. Conversations – with or without any recognisable words – flow in these circumstances.

Southlands Crèche – in the example overleaf and elsewhere in the book – uses toward-facing buggies for babies and toddlers up to about 18 months of age. Older toddlers, who will usually have moved into the next crèche age group, are encouraged to walk short distances. When they use buggies, these are outward-facing, so that toddlers can see directly what is coming up on the trip that day. I agree with this switch to outward-facing buggies, since toddlers and young children need to see around them and to spot interesting sights that are coming into view.

Getting out and about with babies

Babies and young toddlers are fascinated by the sights and sounds of the natural world and, with a little bit of care, they can be taken out and about into the local neighbourhood. Such outings are enjoyable for everyone and, literally, open the door on new conversations and good reasons for toddlers to ask, 'what's that?' or possibly, 'wassat?'.

Committed early years practitioners make sure to get babies and very young children out into the neighbourhood and the natural world, understanding that first-hand experiences are a more powerful way for young children to learn about the world, and build the associated vocabulary, than depending on indoor resources. Good quality books and visual materials are a valuable supplement, and often provoke comments and memories from older toddlers and twos. However, they will not substitute for the direct experiences that provide meaning to the words.

As well as spending time with teams committed to getting out and about, I also appreciate the insights from conversations with two childminders in the Charlton area of south London. Kate and Linda had been actively involved in the development of the Greenwich Forest School project in their neighbourhood.

WHAT ARE CHILDREN LEARNING?

The Rumpus Drop-in group goes out once a week with babies, toddlers and their parents to different parts of the local neighbourhood. The toddlers were fascinated by the natural world of tree trunks, little slopes, leaves, snails, trees to hide behind – everything. There were easy opportunities for communication, but you could also reflect on what other areas of learning were supported for the toddlers in this example.

At one point Lesley (the drop-in leader) found a feather. She held it up high, so the children could see clearly, then dropped it and watched as it floated down. Several children watched intently, including Alan (15½ months). Lesley, and then sometimes a child, picked the feather back up to restart the sequence. Several times Lesley dropped the feather and the children gave a delighted 'weeeee'. They then responded to Lesley's, "Where's it gone?" and looked about on the ground. Then they joined in the delighted, "We've found it!".

Of the small group, Alan was especially excited, stamping his feet with enthusiasm. He seemed to like to see the effect of the wind on the feather. Even after the other children had moved to something else of interest, Alan was still busy looking, finding and handing the feather back to Lesley.

- They were already committed to getting out with their children on a daily basis into the local open spaces. Getting the very youngest children out on a regular basis is partly about attitudes: when practitioners value all the learning from outdoors, then they make it happen.

- They pointed out that it is inevitably time-consuming to get Babies/young toddlers all ready to get out, especially in cold weather, wrapping up warmly. It was important to see this time as part of the routine and not a reason to avoid going outside, and losing the valuable experiences that follow.

- There will often be paths within the more organised landscape of urban parks. However, the less organised outdoor world is often not easily accessible with a buggy. The point of the Forest School experience was that wooded and other natural areas are enjoyed.

Kate and Linda had successfully taken babies as young as 8 and 9 months with them into their wooded Forest School site. Sometimes babies could travel on an adult's back, in a suitable carrier; sometimes they were carried in an adult's arms. A small amount of planning meant that even babies could enjoy the experience. A rug or similar covering enabled babies to be safe on the forest floor. Adults with natural materials sat with them.

Physical development

If all goes well and normal over the first year of life, babies make breathtaking progress in their ability to control their own body and to move themselves around a familiar environment. Babies show an individual pattern in their physical development, as in other areas of their learning.

Some babies are livelier from the beginning, but human babies are very motivated to use their current physical skills and bodily strength to the best of their ability. Babies and young children have a biological drive to be active. It takes active discouragement, through unwise adult actions, to stop lively physical activity.

Babies need to be able to move

Babies initially have limited active control over their arms and legs. They need to be supported in your arms because they cannot hold themselves upright. Their head is relatively large and heavy, in proportion to the rest of their body. Over the early weeks and months their muscle control moves from the top of the body downwards and from the midline of their body outwards. Keen babies try to lift their head before their neck is strong enough to sustain a steady posture. So they tend

to wobble and possibly bang onto your nose when you are holding them close to your face. However, they steadily build stronger muscles by their willingness to keep trying.

Young babies experiment with a wide range of movements, some of which are random and involuntary at the outset. Then repetition means that they begin to build on the unintended consequences of a kick, a wave, a push. They make deliberate actions and you notice more control.

The more a baby is enabled to move, the more they become able to make their body do what they want. Actual physical action sends messages to the baby's brain and repeated actions become laid down as a neural pathway.

Enthusiasm to 'do it again' is perfect for brain development and babies are natural repeaters. For instance, watch a baby who is keen to repeat actions like reaching out and grabbing, or dropping items. You will notice how quickly they become confident and their actions move smoothly, as well as obvious improvement in coordinating what their eyes see with what their limbs do. By happy repetition, babies learn that if they do the same action to the same item, then it usually leads to the same result.

- Over her early months, Tanith liked to be cuddled up close. She was at ease with the momentum of being moved around against my chest secure in a baby carrier.

- Like all babies, in the earliest weeks, her movements looked random. Yet she had a firm grip and would hold tight to a finger. By 7-8 weeks Tanith was very active, working on her muscle control and able to move her head. She struggled to move her whole body and moved hands and feet vigorously.

- Over her third month her kicking became so vigorous that she was able to kick her baby shawl off her legs. She was now able to shift from a position of lying on her side to move onto her back.

- She liked to be helped in vigorous movements and her first loud, throaty laugh came when at 4-5 months, she was enjoying a game with her father. Tanith was laid on her back and Lance lifted her arms up and down in a friendly, repetitive exercise movement.

- Over her fifth month, Tanith was able to bash toys, sometimes off the edge of the tray on her seat. She liked lying on her back on a blanket and developed a two- and one-handed grip for rattles. She also used her fingers to touch and scrabble at anything of interest, including faces.

Experiencing movement with you

Babies need to have plenty of ordinary, happy experience of recognising the messages of their own body. This proprioceptive feedback – direct physical sensations and making sense of them – is also active when you create the movement for a baby.

- Long before babies can choose to rock to and fro themselves, they enjoy this sensation, cuddled in your arms, as you rock gently.

- A slightly different rocking movement is possible when you have a baby lying along the upper half of your legs. Depending on your own physical agility, this experience can be easier to provide when you are sitting on a chair of suitable height.

  - The baby's feet are towards your body and you can create a gentle rocking/bouncing motion as well as moving their arms if they enjoy that. Singing is optional – watch and see what this baby likes best.

PARTNERSHIP WITH PARENTS: ADULTS AS 'EQUIPMENT'

Parents and other family members need to see early years practitioners set a good example of how to support babies' growing physical skills and the enthusiastic mobility of toddlers.

There is good reason to be concerned about the sedentary habits of some older children, whose early experiences did not encourage them to be physically active. Yet in very early childhood, playful adults can help to establish with babies and toddlers the enjoyable habit of being active.

Familiar adults are the best equipment for supporting a great deal of physical movement. Babies feel safe in your arms, as you rock them and gently sway from side to side.

You judge from the baby's reaction when to make more vigorous movements, such as spinning slowly around or doing a seesaw motion with an older baby who can sit securely on the floor, facing you.

From about the middle of the baby year, babies start to have the strength in their legs to stand on your lap, held by their hands or arms. Then you become their human gym, as they bend and bounce using their legs, knees and feet. Babies really enjoy this; you have to ensure they do not bang into your face.

- Long before they can shift their position by bending their knees, let alone jumping, you can give them the up-and-down sensation when you lift them up and down in your arms.

- A baby's key person, and then a few familiar other adults in a nursery, get to know individual babies.

  - Some babies definitely let you know that they like these movements to be more vigorous than another baby of a similar age.

  - You adjust what you do to the wishes of this baby, communicated by their body language and sound making.

- When you dance with a baby in your arms, he or she experiences the gentle twirls and shifts of perspective – back and forth.

  - Again, individual babies will let you know how lively they like this dancing experience to be.

LOOKING CLOSELY AT ONES

Lucy, at 5 months of age, could hold her head and shoulders securely and was happy to sit with support on a lap.

She vocalised with a stream of sound, communicating a range of likely feelings.

- Lucy kicked her legs strongly, one at a time and had a tough grip with her fingers. She liked to hold tight onto an adult thumb.

- Lucy could lie on her stomach and lift her head a bit. But for now, she seemed to be more comfortable on her back. She was happy in a preferred position and made it clear when she had had enough of lying on her stomach.

- Lucy liked to lie on her back on the mat, looking at mobiles, which dangle above.

    ○ She was energetic and moved her legs and trunk.

- She was able to move herself across the mat by rotating a bit each time. Lucy made progress by vigorous movements. She had honed a kind of 'humping' motion, by working her feet and humping her stomach.

- Lucy was close to turning over on her side but not yet. She seemed to be trying to lever a bit of her legs.

- She also was able to lift both feet up to right angles, bending at the waist.

    ○ She was energetic, with lively full body movements, working both arms and her legs together.

When I saw Lucy again at 7 months, she was very confident on a lap and was able to bend forward and back again from her sitting position – still held safely by an adult's arms.

I held a fluffy animal for her to see. Lucy leaned forward, using both hands to explore this new toy. The animal's head tucked in when the magnetised tail was brought forwards.

Lucy watched me tuck in the head, and then open it up again, three times. Then she put out her hand and closed the head down herself. She looked at me expectantly and I opened it up, then she closed it down, repeating this sequence several times.

Time on the floor

There are times when it is wise to have babies secure in a proper seat. They can gain from being able to see what is going on and are safe on the move, such as when travelling in a car.

However, it is not beneficial for babies to spend hours in a seat – either because of a family pattern that involves continual driving about or unresolved concerns about babies in a busy nursery environment.

Babies need to have generous time for their physical explorations. They are finding out all about:

- Where do I end and other people start?

- What's that? Is that my hand, how do I make it work like that?

- Is that my foot? Where's it gone now?

- How did I do that? Can I do it again?

Babies need plenty of time on a comfortable, flat surface like the floor. You make it a pleasant place with soft coverings and an area that is not a thoroughfare for adults or mobile young children. Babies are secure on this comfortable base, with you beside them.

- Babies can lie on their back looking up or across at you. If you are close by, then your face and interaction makes this interesting.

- A place for babies on their back can be made interesting with mobiles, some of which can be created by you – not all bought items.

- Babies experience a variety of sensations from their own body. They are able to wave arms and legs vigorously. They experience a firm, but comfortable base as they wriggle or move their head to and fro.

- When they are able to squirm and push against the floor, babies are able to lever themselves to the side. This large movement is not possible if they are secured in a baby seat.

When babies are sleeping in their cot, then for safety, they should be placed on their back and not their stomach. This advice is supported by research to reduce the risk of unexplained death of infants whilst sleeping in their cot.

However, this sound advice about sleeping position is not applicable to when older babies are fully awake. Babies, whose muscle control has reached their shoulders, can be placed on their stomachs for short periods of time. These are babies who are now able to lift their face and part of their upper body off the surface.

- From this position, babies can stretch their legs, arms and spine in safe ways. They are able to strengthen the muscles in their neck and shoulders and continue the progress of increasing control down their body.

- Of course you do not leave babies in this position when they are clearly letting you know they have had enough for now. Again, if you are on the floor with them, then this position does not feel as if they are alone.

- Try lying out full length, with your face towards the baby. As soon as babies lift their head a little they see you smiling at them. Try lifting the very front part of your body, plus your head, up and down a little, so that you and the baby are making the same movements.

- So long as you are close and observant, babies will not become distressed. You will help them before their sound-making communicates, 'I'm a bit fed up now'.

By the middle of the first year, babies have often gained sufficient upper body strength and control to be able to sit securely without toppling sideways. Of course, you do not

PARTNERSHIP WITH PARENTS: USING THE FLOOR

Reflect on how you can share anecdotes with parents/carers about their baby's floor time.

Also share the developmental good sense of enabling babies from 3-4 months to lie, freely moving, on the floor.

- What is this baby able to do on the floor that is impossible in a seat?

- If you care for babies who have spent hours so far in their seat, then do not give up at the first attempt. Being unsecured may initially feel like an odd sensation to this baby.

- Make sure you are on the floor as well – stretch out for your full length, just like the baby.

- Make this time personal and full of friendly communication.

- By all means have one or two play items that you know this baby will like – but not lots. You are the most encouraging play resource in this situation.

LOOKING CLOSELY AT ONES

In the Rumpus Drop-in, Marie (4½ months) was happy lying on her tummy, arms tucked under her body. She could hold her head and shoulders secure and up.

She looked comfortable and was busy looking alertly around. Sometimes she moved her head from side to side.

Marie especially liked lying on the shiny blue Lycra® stretch of material.

Marie also spent some time lying on her back. In this position she looked to the right, where a black and white tin seemed to have caught her attention. Her mother said that Marie had managed to turn herself for the first time last week from this position. Her expression had communicated that Marie had surprised herself.

Marie spent time looking at the set of three black and white tins. She was also pulling at her bib with one hand and sucking her fingers. At one point her mother held a chain in front of Marie and then let it rattle on the tin. Marie looked alert and watching. On her tummy, Marie could pull her legs up to her body.

LOOKING CLOSELY AT ONES

In the Rumpus Drop-in, Jamie (6 months) was able to sit securely, with a slight lean against his mother's knees.

He was able to lean out, pick up a willow ball and get it back to himself. His technique was to pull with one hand and then a two-handed grasp and then bring the ball to his mouth.

Jamie put the willow ball to one side and leant forward to touch the collection of pebbles. Then he returned to holding the ball. His mother offered him the basket full of the wooden solid shapes (rather like a mini skittle). Jamie still held onto the willow but was able also to suck on a peg, then bang the ball with the solid peg.

Lesley (the drop-in leader) gave Jamie two of the tin lids and he banged the two together to make a noise. Then Jamie had one peg shape in each hand and was rooting around in the basket, which his mother held steady and close for him. Jamie looked and selected in deliberate way – sucking the rounded end of one peg, feeling for and then discarding another peg in the basket. Lesley then moved a treasure basket close and Jamie pulled out a large-scale bead necklace, followed by the soft purse as well.

Jamie was held by his mother, close to a really large teddy placed by the sofa. He was interested in this teddy (larger than him), touching it and vocalising.

His mother then put Jamie on his stomach. He was able to put his hands flat on floor, so that his legs came up a bit. He stretched, pulled a tin lid forwards and examined it. With just a little bit of help from his mother, Jamie got hold of one of the black and white tins, pulled it towards himself and mouthed it.

Later his mother settled Jamie in the crescent-shaped support cushion. He picked up an oblong tin and used two hands to explore. Jamie managed to hold the tin, explore it by mouthing and then vocalise to his mother.

He was also keen to pull at the shiny blue Lycra® too. At one point, Jamie was busy holding the Lycra, mouthing the wooden mini skittle shape and vocalising – all at the same time.

Think about what Jamie was discovering during this relaxed time of exploratory play. What kind of skills was he using and in what ways was he probably working on and extending those skills. How was he using his senses to learn about and make sense of his immediate world?

rush this development: you look with care to be sure that the baby can support their weight in this way. When babies are close to being able to sit – no slumping – they benefit with a secure half-moon cushion at their back or being able to sit in the circle created by the legs of a sitting adult. The exciting new development for a sitting baby is that their hands are now free. They can use fingers, hands and arms to stretch and get something that is close enough.

The value of crawling

For babies the additional advantage of time on their stomach is that they are in the right position to get into all fours, when they have the muscle strength. Sometimes they will manage to roll over from lying on their back. When they try out the all fours position, then babies start to take some of their weight on their outstretched hands as well as their knees and legs. They work their palms in the full stretch that is necessary to hold their weight in this position, then to rock to and fro and finally to learn to crawl. This movement of lifting their body weight off the floor is a natural and positive gymnastic game that helps their spine to become more flexible. The attempts to crawl and then success encourages freedom of movement in the joints and builds up strength in babies' arms and legs.

The great advantage of crawling, as a form of independent mobility, is that it is a total workout for the body, using both sides in a coordinated movement. Watch a crawling baby and you can observe how each side of their body is used in a smooth action, which brings the right arm to move with the left leg and the left arm with the right leg. Once a baby is a confident crawler, this complex coordinated motion is undertaken with impressive speed.

Babies combine the vital information from their hands, and often also from knees and feet to create a familiar sensation of what crawling feels like. They experience the sense of stillness and of motion. But they also use vision – looking down at the floor sometimes, but also they look ahead into the distance of the room or across the grass outdoors. They gain valuable experience of checking what they see against where they are and where they plan to reach.

Once babies are poised to crawl, their best supporting equipment is a familiar adult, who is close and in a similar position on the floor to the baby. You provide company, as well as the visual message that it is enjoyable to be here.

- Move an object slightly closer to a child to encourage that stretch or effort to move independently. Do not always hand it over, but obviously do not hold back so much that a baby is frustrated or distressed.

- Let babies experience a bit of frustration. A baby who is moved straightaway does not learn to persevere in an attempt to move themselves.

- If a baby is really struggling to get into a forward crawl, then try giving them a firm support by placing your hands against their feet. You do not push the baby; you let the baby push against your hands.

- Be willing to crawl after the child – in a game of crawling-chasing. Act as an item of on-all-fours equipment that will provide under, round and nose-to-nose encounters.

- Crawl together through a tunnel, if you have one, or under lightweight material, like organza. And do keep going with these lively physical games into the toddler year.

Given the chance, most babies will spend time crawling before walking. Yet, even when babies did not spend so much time in baby seats, some of them went straight into walking. Babies who choose to miss out the crawling stage will still enjoy, and benefit from, games of crawling around with a playful adult. In your partnership with parents, it is important to highlight what babies gain by plenty of crawling time.

You need to deal, if necessary, with the unhelpful idea that early walking is a preferable developmental pattern or indicates a more impressive baby. Some babies are securely upright and walking by 10 or 11 months. However, there is no reason for concern about mobile older babies or young toddlers whose physical independence does not yet include steady walking. It is not a competition, and some parents may welcome reassurance that their active baby is doing

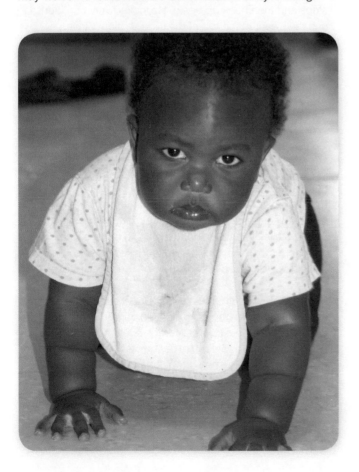

LOOKING CLOSELY AT ONES

- By her seventh month, Tanith was able to cover a short distance, starting from lying on her back. A vigorous humping movement meant that she travelled backwards in this way, her face still upwards.

- Placed on her stomach, she was now able to get into the crawling position, although not to make any progress in movement. Her legs were strong and she loved to stand, with her arms held, and to bend her knees in order to bounce and weave about on the spot.

- By her eighth month she was confident in her sitting position and able to twist, lunge for something of interest and return to a stable sitting position ready to explore what she had grabbed.

- She liked very much to seize our outstretched hands and pull herself strongly up to a standing position. She also liked to stand supporting herself with both hands flat on the low and very stable coffee table.

- Over the next few weeks she steadily mastered the ability to pull herself up from a seated position and over her ninth month practised the art of cruising along the furniture, shifting her hand holds as she went.

- Over her eighth month, Tanith had steadily mastered the business of crawling. At the beginning of the month she could get into the hands-and-knees crawling position and was able to rock herself to and fro vigorously. She would then look up with a surprised expression on her face, as if to say, 'I've done so much moving! Why am I still in the same place?'.

  ○ By mid-month she had perfected a kind of combination crawl and stomach squirm. Initially, Tanith succeeded only in moving backwards. Her facial expression and stream of sounds told us clearly that she was very annoyed about this situation.

  ○ Over the next few days her focus on practice was impressive and very soon she managed her first forward crawl. A couple of repetitions and Tanith perfected the style. From then on, she never went backwards, unless that movement was intentional.

- Using hands, knees and legs, offers older babies a very efficient way of getting around independently. Tanith did not learn to walk until 13 months of age, yet she was speedy in moving about her home in purposeful physical movement.

just fine. It is a different matter if you have an older baby who shows little or no interest in trying to move at all.

Physical ways of exploring the world

In the first year of life, babies are motivated to use their current physical skills to the full. The larger, whole-body movements are just as important as the smaller-scale, fine movements.

Once older babies are mobile, you will observe them bottom-shuffle or crawl to get themselves closer to something of interest. Then, having shifted into the sitting position, their hands are free to get busy.

At different points over their first year, you will notice that individual babies have a favourite way of connecting physically with items in their familiar environment. They will persevere in using this approach, as the way to learn more about their world. These persistent ways of behaving are called schemas. In the baby year you will observe schemas of single physical actions, rather than the sequences (like transporting items) that become possible in the toddler year.

Look out for these physical schemas over the first year and encourage parents, through anecdotes about their baby, to value these important developments.

- **Mouthing and sucking:** Babies explore by putting objects to their mouths and continue to use this method into the second year of life. The nerve endings of a baby's lips, mouth and tongue are the most sensitive in their body. So, they are using the most effective means to play and learn.

- **Holding:** Very young babies have to put all their energy into combining vision and stretch to get hold of an interesting object or part of a person. Initially they cannot easily open their grasp to let go again. So, if they have got hold of your hair or that of another child, you often have to undo their grasp. Once they can hold tight to an item of interest, they can also wave it to and fro.

- **Inspecting:** Once babies can hold and look, they often stare at an object of interest. They may look at what appear to be very minor details, but everything is new to them. Continued experience is needed before objects and people become familiar.

- **Hitting:** Babies now have greater physical control and can follow through by looking. So they can connect with an object or substance with more energy. They may tap at a teddy or pat down on a wet surface on their highchair.

- **Shaking:** The ability to hold tight and then make movement allows babies to move an object from side to side. Perhaps

it makes a noise, like a rattle or material cubes with bells inside. Then the pleasure of making something happen encourages babies to repeat the action.

  - Their physical ability enables them to explore cause-and-effect at a simple and intriguing level.

- **Examining:** Once babies become able to use both hands and to shift their grip, they can examine in detail. Babies

LOOKING CLOSELY AT ONES

Babies who have had generous time for physical activity become stable toddlers who move independently and with confidence. In the Rumpus Drop-in, Steven (19 months) used the full opportunities of the indoor clambering equipment.

I watched as he stood on the middle platform and hooked his hands and arms over the railings and leaned backwards a little. I was sitting at the base of one of the exits (a set of steps) and Steven stood looking at me in a meaningful way. I said: "Am I in your way? Do you want to come down the stairs?". Steven indicated 'yes' and I moved.

Steven used the handrail to come down the short set of steps and then back up again. He looked very confident and then went to the top of the slide section. Steven showed that he knew not to try to walk down the slide. He sat and then lay on his stomach – trying to turn so as to go down legs first and on his tummy. But he could not quite line himself up. His mother helped Steven with the final turn and down he went.

Steven was speedily up the steps again and this time succeeded in turning himself and pushing until he tipped into the right position to slide down the slide. Once again he climbed the steps, crawling through the tunnel section. Now he looked very sure of the movement: rotating on his tummy and feeling for the right position with his feet. Even if Steven turned his head, he could not see if he was properly lined up; he had to feel it. He now had his technique well honed and did the sequence twice more.

Steven had out of choice gained a lot of experience with this equipment. At one point he tried carefully to stand upright in the tunnel but realised he could not and did not bang his head. Steven experimented with coming down the steps in a semi-jump, holding onto the rail at the side, moving his body as if to jump then sort of slide, both feet together down. He held himself steady with this chosen technique for the three steps. Then he repeated this sequence twice more.

become interested in moving an object, taking a close look, and perhaps a poke, from different angles. Babies become more able to manipulate an object so that they can turn or push it around.

- **Tearing:** Babies who manage to explore paper objects may discover the delights of tearing. This action provides a mixture of sound and interesting cause-and-effect. Tearing is often combined with a scrunching and bashing action, which also looks very satisfying to the baby.

- **Rubbing:** Babies become interested in texture and may move a soft toy or piece of material against their cheek or mouth. By bringing the item close to their face, some babies appear to get some more information, as well as enjoy the sensation.

- **Dropping:** Babies' ability to grasp, let go and track with their eyes adds the intriguing possibility of dropping objects. This action is even more interesting to do from a height as that adds a noise.

- **Throwing:** Babies' physical skills continue to develop until they can manage the complex sequence of holding something and then combining the throwing and letting go actions.

Once older babies have achieved physical control over a number of ways to manipulate objects, they no longer restrict

themselves to same physical action/schema. You will notice that they try several different approaches to the same item. They are able to combine different actions in a deliberate sequence, such as grasping hold of something, mouthing it for a while, then turning it around and maybe dropping or throwing it.

Physically adept toddlers

Once young toddlers have confident control and mobility, then you can see how they repeat sequences of action out of choice and sometimes they persist, for some time, in a particular way of exploring and organising their world. These repeated patterns are more complex schemas than those you can observe with babies.

LOOKING CLOSELY AT ONES

In the World of Discovery session at Sure Start Tilbury, Angie (10 months) sat securely for a long time, exploring different items within her reach, one at a time in the order that she chose to pull them into her lap. Angie spent a while with a black and white circle with a busy pattern that had been laminated. This resource bent easily in her hands and she was busy waving it about and moving it from one hand to the other.

Then Angie pulled in a length of white plastic chain, which she rattled and pulled, with a strong hold on different parts of the chain. Then she grasped a black quilted oven glove. First she held tight onto the glove, then Angie put it on her head, took it off, shook it well and threw it. She then returned to her investigation of the laminated design. Unexpectedly, it flew out of her hands and Angie moved quickly from her sitting position to a semi all-fours to reach out, grasp the laminate, pull it back and settle herself back into the sitting position.

Later Angie had the lid of a black and white box and was pretending to give it. That is the only word to use, since Angie gave all the signals that this was a teasing kind of play. She offered the lid to her mother, her mother said 'ta', yet Angie held on tight. The look on her face really did suggest that this action was deliberate. Then Angie repeated the same pattern with another adult.

Angie did a lot of holding items up to show, seeking acknowledgment from the nearest adult – her mother and then me – before selecting another item. She managed to get her sock off, held it up for my approval and then explored it. Rather like with the oven glove, Angie felt the sock, rubbed it over her head and right to the back of her neck and then back to the front again.

Perhaps an individual toddler becomes very interested in filling up containers with different items, possibly carrying these around from place to place. Another toddler, with or without a friend, may become absorbed day after day in covering and uncovering himself or play items, in wrapping paper or cloth around toys or his own feet. Attentive adults will be able to see problem solving around cause and effect, materials that fit and those that do not, materials that operate as effective wraps or covers and those that are just not up to the job. These toddlers' physical skills are being put to purposeful use in ways that support their learning about their world and the basic grasp of a range of mathematical concepts as well.

Nurture and healthy habits

Familiar adults are fully responsible for taking good care of babies and toddlers. Early childhood is the best time to build healthy habits for food, drink, physical exercise and getting enough rest and sleep. However, babies and very young children are utterly dependent on the quality of nurture provided by their family and early years practitioners.

Healthy children need to be physically active, out of choice. Unless they are prevented, babies are keen to be busy with their hands, legs and whole bodies. It takes seriously unwise adult behaviour to block this physical enthusiasm over

the baby and toddler months – let alone to produce sedentary older children who no longer choose to engage in physical play.

Nutritious food and drink will prime baby and toddler taste buds, without the over stimulation of highly processed foods. Good nutrition, including appropriate drinks, builds healthy bones and fuels growing. However, sufficient rest and sleep is also important.

Like food, you develop healthy routines in partnership with parents, aiming for continuity with the family pattern. You will have to talk the issues through with a parent, if you have good reason to be concerned that parents' preference would unbalance their young child's diet or require them to go without a much-needed nap.

A high value for caring and a nurturing environment is a non-negotiable part of best practice over early childhood. Care has to be integrated with support for very young learning, through active respect for the personal care of babies and toddlers and protecting time for the regular routines of a day. Older babies and the toddlers are keen to share in their own care, within the limits of their current physical skills.

LOOKING CLOSELY AT ONES

Buckingham's Nursery offers full day care from the baby year. My observations in the different age-based rooms showed how this learning journey is steadily supported. I watched many instances of these appropriate early experiences.

Sitting babies enjoyed sand in a tuff spot on the floor. They chose to sit right in the sand, poke and explore the texture. Adults helped them with the sieves – putting sand in one and shaking it free, as a baby looked. Babies looked happy as they felt the sand with their hands and their toes.

Toddlers enjoyed the 'Shake Boxes', borrowed from the Tweenies room (twos). These very young children were interested in the contents of the boxes (covered with shiny wrapping paper). They focused on getting items out and putting them back – several times. There was a great deal of deliberate physical activity and concentration by toddlers: feeling items, grasping the different kinds of materials, feeling around in the boxes.

At other times I watched several babies and toddlers with play materials where they could take items out of a container and then put them back in again – often many times. They lifted up flaps or little 'doors' and worked hard to get items in or out – sometimes without success.

An emotionally warm environment and patient adults encourage young toddlers to want to help out generally in a home-like nursery, just as in a family home. Older toddlers become adept with a small dustpan and brush and wield a damp cloth with style for wiping up a table. Apart from a genuine support of their physical skills, these joint domestic activities lay a firm foundation for later practical life skills – plus a positive outlook that the grown-ups do not do all the work around here.

Best early years practice rests on commitment to a caring, personal relationship between individual babies or toddlers and their key person, or childminder. The 'key person approach' (Lindon, 2010) applies across early childhood, but in very early childhood it is closely linked with babies' and toddlers' need for intimate physical care. Although even young babies will often try to hold a bottle or wave around a spoon, they do not yet have the physical agility to deal with any of their own personal care.

In terms of best practice, your awareness of babies' limited physical skills links with a full understanding that their emotional security and well-being depend very much upon practitioners' commitment to care and caring. There are a lot of nappies to change and a lot of baby clothes to wash, or put for washing. There are lots of bottles of milk to give to babies, or your working in partnership so that the baby's mother can breast feed for part of the day.

Early years practice that truly supports babies – such as I saw in the settings described in this book – values the personal care routines, gives time to them and views nappy changing or feeding as intimate times for communication, just as much as excellent physical care. It is poor practice for practitioners to think of such times as less important than play, or for anyone for believe that there are long parts of a day with babies or young toddlers when 'nothing' is happening because the adult is focussed on nappies, bottles or bowls of pureed vegetables.

Best early years practice is established when there is no artificial boundary between what is called 'care' and what gets labelled as 'education'. Babies and young toddlers, who experience personal and communicative times of care, are relaxed and ready to get back to their crawling games or get their hands back into the water play. Equally, babies and toddlers who have learned that nappy changing time is chatting time with their key person, are far less put out by realising that for the moment the book with the lovely pictures has been put to one side and they are being gently undressed on the changing table.

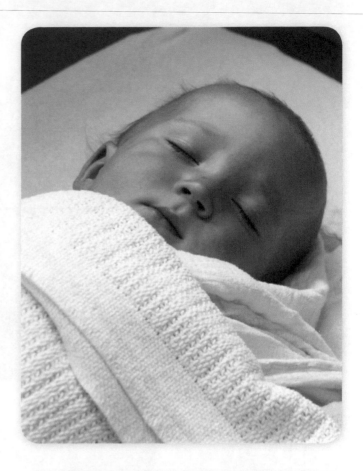

LOOKING CLOSELY AT ONES

Best early years practice is that time is given for meals, because this part of the day is respected as valuable. In the baby room of Southlands Crèche, I watched as one practitioner was sitting close to two babies who were each sitting in a high chair, enjoying their lunch. She alternated her attention between the babies, making it a personal time for each one. She helped them as appropriate and commented on what they were doing and enjoying eating.

In Grove House Infant and Toddler Centre, the key person remained close to their key babies and toddlers over mealtimes. Flexible planning of routines allowed for the reality that young babies were not necessarily eating at the same time as everyone else. Practitioners fed babies who are unable yet to feed themselves. But the key person provided babies with the means to feed themselves. They had finger food as appropriate and encouragement to pick up and get food to their mouth.

In both Southlands and Grove House, older babies had their own spoon and the chance to get some food in their mouth. They were supported by the key person with another spoon. In each setting, generous time is given for mealtimes, as an important part of the day. There is no temptation to think, 'It's quicker or less messy if I do it'.

Literacy

Babies and young toddlers are at the very beginning of their learning journey towards literacy. Developmentally appropriate experiences now will make a positive difference for later learning. Firm foundations for later literacy are built from enjoyable experiences for babies and toddlers that fit their age and understanding.

Happy communication and conversational exchanges support babies' move towards spoken language. Much further along the developmental path, it will be hard going for children to learn the written version of any language, unless they have a large working vocabulary and confidence in their oral language(s). All the examples in the section on 'Communication and Language' illustrate the many ways that communicative and familiar adults support this process.

First steps on a long journey

A genuine enjoyment of books can start in the baby year, so that even young toddlers show they have favourite books and the simple narratives that are part of some rhymes. Babies' interest in books is supported by personal times with a familiar adult. As often as possible this will be a one-to-one, but a cosy time can also work with one adult and two older babies, who are secure with that adult in a large comfortable chair or a sofa.

LOOKING CLOSELY AT ONES

Babies and toddlers do not benefit from being organised into group story time; they are far too young. Best early years practice is that practitioners respond spontaneously to non-verbal requests from older babies and toddlers. During my time in Buckingham's Nursery, I regularly saw practitioners respond promptly to the interest of a baby or toddler to share a book.

I watched one practitioner sitting in a comfortable corner with a young toddler on her lap. They were looking together at a flap book, taking the simple story line one page at a time. The adult made brief and relevant comments like: "Who's hiding behind the door?". The toddler had a teddy with her and the adult asked at one point: "Shall Teddy have a peek?". Teddy did have a look. Another young toddler came to join the pair. He was welcomed and was able to look into the little mirror that was part of the page.

Older babies and toddlers show how they relish the illustrations in books but also the simple storylines, especially those with a repeating phrase. Toddlers can follow a simple pattern in a story, or a consistent commentary that you make to an illustrated book without written text. Your words and gestures provoke their developing imagination and they like favourites again and again. The repetition helps young children to learn and then recognise familiar tales.

Toddlers start to chime in with repeated lines and have a go at the gestures. Early experience with books creates older toddlers who start to tell stories to themselves using familiar story phrases, even your pacing and intonation for this narrative. It is important to tell a story in the same way each time, or with only very minor changes. Toddlers and any young children like to have familiar stories told 'properly'. Their facial expressions and words start to communicate not only, 'what will happen next?', but also 'when will we get to the bit I like about...?'.

Sounds and rhythm

Babies around the world relish being sung to by familiar adults. Babies like a rhythmic flow to spoken language and they are very responsive to musical tones.

Nursery rhymes and chants support babies to listen, follow the flow of the song and to join in as far as they are able. The slightly exaggerated pattern of nursery rhymes helped to attune babies' recognition of the sounds of their familiar language(s).

Babies are born attuned to musical rhythm as well as the sound of the human voice. They really do appear to have an innate sensitivity to music and tuneful singing – that is to say they are born with this ability. In the final months before birth, babies can hear sounds from 'outside' and they show a reaction of familiarity to songs that they can only have heard while 'inside'.

Babies show an active interest in songs and rhymes long before they can actually join in. Watch out for that sparkle of recognition on a baby's face as you sing the opening lines of a rhyme or song that has become familiar. You are the best source of singing and babies will never criticise the quality of your voice.

- Build on the trills of sound that babies make spontaneously, as they move from single sound making into repetitive, self-made tunefulness. Repeat back some of the baby's tuneful sound streams and see the smile.

- Be ready to comfort an uneasy baby or fretful toddler with tuneful humming. This merging of gentle talk and semi-singing can be very reassuring to a baby or young toddler, often combined with gentle rocking in the cradle of your arms or your lap.

- Peaceful singing and lullabies are not only positive for babies. Days with very young children are physically and

---

PARTNERSHIP WITH PARENTS: APPROPRIATE RESOURCES

There is now a large number of commercial toys, targeted at the baby and toddler years, which are plastered with single letters and claim to support very early learning.

However, babies and toddlers are still busy working out that people and familiar objects have names, which can be said out loud. The symbolic nature of letters – and the numbers which are often also on these plastic or soft toys – means nothing at all to them. If adults have very limited understanding of the learning journey towards literacy, it may seem a good choice to buy such toys.

Early years practitioners have a professional responsibility to keep their knowledge of child development well refreshed. It is crucial that parents are not given misleading messages through the resources they see in your home as a childminder or your nursery.

Likewise, you need to think always of the message given by what you fix to the walls. You provide a distorted view of the learning journey towards literacy, if letter friezes dominate in a room for babies or toddlers. The same point applies if your provision is for slightly older children, whose disabilities mean their development is at a younger stage.

LOOKING CLOSELY AT ONES

Babies are happy to be part of enjoying a book with an older child. This example was in a family home, but I have seen similar enjoyable events within nurseries when babies and young children have time together.

At 5 months of age Lucy is already aware of Thomas the Tank Engine, because this character is a firm favourite of her older sister, Sophie (2yrs, 8mths). During one of my visits, Lucy spent time staring at the Thomas DVD and homed in visually on different parts of the picture.

On another visit, I watched as Lucy enjoyed *Rumble in the Jungle* (Orchard, 1998); a book that Sophie had chosen and her mother, Louise, was reading to them both. Sophie was happy for Lucy to be part of the experience and keen to point out some of the animals to her baby sister. Lucy stared intently at the book and touched each page as Louise turned it.

emotionally tiring. A time to sit in peace, rocking a young toddler and singing, is also relaxing for the adult.

● Suitable songs for older babies and toddlers often come with hand movements, whether done by the singer or gently done to the child.

You get to know individuals, so of course you adjust the liveliness to what you now know this baby relishes.

You can be creative, and accessorise any song that a baby or toddler likes with your own special bounces, tickles or helping the baby with arm or leg movements. You come equipped with all that is necessary: arms to hold gently but securely, a firm lap and bendy knees.

● Be ready to repeat favourites many times and realise that, once you have added the new movements, you have to recall them in detail. This pattern is now an essential part of the song, as far as this baby or toddler is concerned.

● Once a song, rhyme or piece of music becomes familiar, young toddlers will make their own request by word or gesture. Soon they will sing parts of the song.

● Young children are very open-minded, they like anything you sing with enthusiasm and obvious enjoyment: nursery rhymes, popular current songs or older songs like 'Daisy Daisy'.

LOOKING CLOSELY AT ONES

In Buckingham's Nursery I saw many instances of spontaneous singing with the babies and toddlers, as well as cosy times when a very small group enjoyed snuggling up for several songs. Practitioners were swift to tune into babies and toddlers and acknowledge the sounds they chose to make, such as patting the table, bringing their fists together or making a clapping movement.

Familiar adults followed the lead of babies or toddlers and joined in their play with sound makers. The key person often commented on what a baby or toddler was doing at that moment, for instance: "Are you banging?" when a baby was making a noise with a simple instrument.

The team at Buckinghams were very attentive to what had caught the babies' attention. The practitioners also adjusted the pace and volume of singing or sound making to what babies showed they enjoyed. The singing was a personal experience; even in the small group coming together to sing all the babies were close to an adult and enjoyed eye contact as well as touch for the hand movements of some songs.

PARTNERSHIP WITH PARENTS: SHARING SONGS

Practitioners and parents do not have to have an identical repertoire. However, it is valuable to have a two-way share over the favourites of a baby or toddler: the special gestures as well as the words.

Extend your repertoire by asking for family favourites from children's parents. You can add songs that are familiar to this family and be ready to learn and practise simple refrains in a language that you do not know, or know well.

Do not be in a rush to provide songs or music from traditions that are unknown to any of the children in your care. Very young children need to become familiar with their own cultural tradition and traditions of 'my friend's family'.

Singing and rhymes, like stories, should be a personal experience for babies and any young children – a time when there is an opportunity for snuggling into a familiar adult. With babies, especially younger babies, many of these spontaneous times will be one-to-one or at most one-to-two. You will get to know individual babies: do they prefer quieter songs more like lullabies or do they like louder parts to a song? Does their expression tell you they now know what is coming?

Making deliberate marks

It will be a long time before little fingers and hands can hold a pencil or make letters. Yet, baby fingers are busy with grasping, picking up and other physical skills that will stand them in good stead for the task of writing in the distant future. For now, suitable resources help older babies to experience meaningful mark making. They are clearly happy to get their hands into semiliquid materials – swirling, poking, wiping. Enthusiastic mark making joins with a pleasure in decisions over what goes where.

Older babies and young toddlers relish big scale movements and getting their hands into paint or similar materials that can be swirled, pulled across paper and sloshed onto a surface. Babies and toddlers clearly have a grand time when they

LOOKING CLOSELY AT ONES

The awareness and enjoyment starts young. I observed several happy sound-making and singing times in Buckingham's Nursery. The babies had an enjoyable time – several of them with two or three adults at one point – with simple shaker and percussion instruments. They showed that they enjoyed the songs and rhymes sung by the adults as they all sat comfortably close together, with babies on a lap whenever they want.

A baby who needed changing was asked and then carried gently to the bathroom, able to take her instrument with her. She came back after her change and was eased back into the cosy singing group and everyone sung the song that this baby had been enjoying during her changing time.

Simple sound makers and basic instruments were often available for babies and toddlers. I watched as individual babies made purposeful movements with items like a tambourine and returned to make the same action with the same item. It really looked as if a baby had understood something of how a sound-making resource worked, had recalled the experience and returned for another go.

From happy sound-making exploration, toddlers show a strong sense of musical rhythm. I sat with one toddler who indicated to me, several times, that she wanted a musical toy wound up. She then swayed in time to the nursery rhyme and moved her hands.

Toddlers in this nursery regularly showed that they recognised some rhymes. They used the appropriate gestures for a rhyme, even when they did not yet sing the words.

get involved in appropriate baby art experiences. There is a happy outcome in terms of personal satisfaction, sensory exploration and deliberate mark making. There is not going to be a neat end-product to give to parents or stick on the wall.

It is crucial that early years practitioners understand, and share with families, how much sitting and crawling babies get out of an activity in which just as much paint gets on the baby as on the roll of paper. Photographs can show the genuine thrill of toddler foot painting and creative piles or collections from a generous store of tubes, shiny pebbles or large corks.

I have been delighted to watch baby and toddler art sessions – in a wide range of settings, not only those mentioned in this book. Wise practitioners make sure there is no rush. Relaxed timing is important for enjoying the art experience itself, but also for less sure babies or toddlers to have the time to look from the sidelines and decide they too would like to have a go. Babies are individuals and not everyone will plunge straight into an unfamiliar activity.

Of course babies and toddlers get as much paint over themselves as on a large sheet of paper. The best approach is to make the clean-up process part of the whole experience. Indoors, or in the garden on a warm day, I have watched babies and toddlers have just as much fun sitting in a baby bath of warm water (or similar large container) and splashing with pleasure, as the adult ensures that the paint, cornflour or other substance is steadily removed. Being wrapped in a nice, warm towel, dried and re-dressed is a happy time too.

LOOKING CLOSELY AT ONES

When I visited The Rainbow Centre in Norfolk, the baby room team had recently created a wall display arising from a painting session with the babies. An array of photos showed babies with their hands and feet fully involved in the paint. The images were arranged around a very large sheet of paper on which many babies are chosen to splosh paint and create marks.

It was easy for parents to see how much their baby had enjoyed this full-on art experience. There was no misleading message that any baby had made a conventional and finished 'painting'.

This accurate wall display contrasted with mistaken practice I have encountered sometimes when practitioners have felt intense pressure to produce unrealistic artwork for the wall. The same problem applies when drawings or collages, given to parents to take home, cannot possibly have been done by the babies or toddlers.

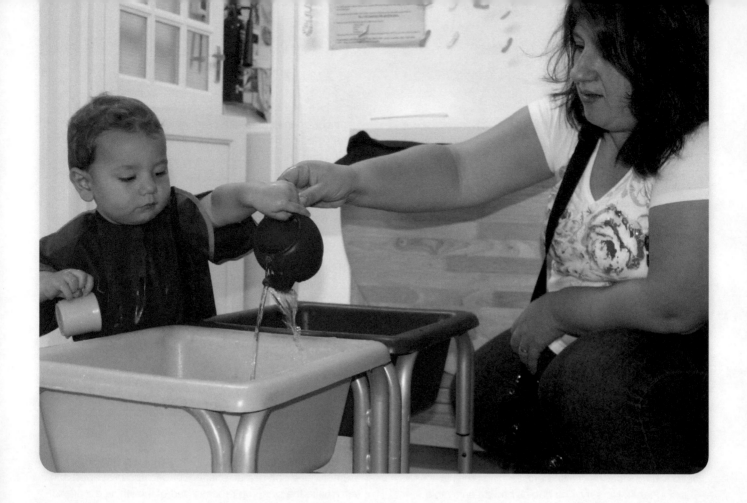

Mathematics

This area of learning focuses on how even young children can develop a secure understanding of amount and basic number, space and shape and simple measurement. Such early mathematical skills may still seem a stretch too far for the world of ones. However, the very beginnings of mathematical understanding are grounded in opportunities for babies and young toddlers to get their hands on a wide range of open-ended materials. Abstract concepts will later make sense to young children, because they have a meaningful and very practical context for understanding ideas like size and shape.

Very early understanding of amounts

Babies and very young toddlers do not understand abstract, written numbers in the sense of 1, 2, 3; so it is pointless, and developmentally misleading, to buy commercial toys, books and wall friezes which feature single written numbers. However, babies notice differences in their familiar world. Their reactions and body language tell you they are aware that something has appeared, or something has gone. Their very early grasp of number is along the lines of, 'that's

different', 'something's changed there' and sometimes, 'I wasn't expecting that!'.

There are many good reasons to sing to babies and with toddlers. Singing is an enjoyable form of social communication and helps very young children to tune into the sounds of their language(s). They definitely enjoy the songs and rhymes that include numbers for a good reason: counting up or down about items in the song storyline. Number words operate as a basic ordering of a sequence of actions in a rhyme like 'Round and round the garden'. Babies and toddlers also enjoy number words as part of a singing and action sequence, as in touch and counting toes.

It has been a serious challenge for researchers to demonstrate that babies notice and understand basic amounts, long before they know and use number words. Alison Gopnik (2009) and her colleagues resolved that problem. The research team have shown how older babies not only look very carefully, but also make sense of their observations in terms of 'how much' or 'more' of one thing than another. In one experiment, nine-month-old babies were shown a box full of ping-pong balls, of which 80% were red and 20% were white. Then a screen was put in front of the

PARTNERSHIP WITH PARENTS: REALLY, REALLY EARLY MATHS

Observant adults are alert to the small details of what babies and toddlers do, what interests them and how they get a grip, usually in a very literal way, on the world around them.

Very young children make explorations and come to their own conclusions about their world. They are already aware of number or shape at the most basic, visual, get-my-hands-on-it level. It is so important that early years practitioners respect these beginnings to mathematical understanding as the real thing. You can then share individual anecdotes with parents and other family carers.

Nobody should be waiting; thinking that nothing is going to happen in this area of learning for a very long time.

PARTNERSHIP WITH PARENTS: OBJECT PERMANENCE

Within the second half of the first year, babies reach the significant understanding that objects can go temporarily out of sight, but are not gone for ever. This concept of object permanence is an exciting intellectual step for babies.

It is well worth sharing with parents, if they are not aware, that their baby now looks for something that previously he would have assumed was gone. Perhaps a baby who loves peek-a-boo with a person is now aware that the teddy, hidden by his key person, must be under the cloth. Yet, a month ago, you could hide a ball or other toy in full sight of this baby and he would have ceased to look, once the toy was covered.

This new understanding of the world means that older babies can explore by putting objects into other containers or very simple posting boxes. They know the item is still there, so they search to find it and bring it back out again. Putting things in-and-out again and again gives babies direct experience of fit and relative size.

This development is an example of how you need to make a good guess about babies' thinking by watching what they do.

box and an adult picked out five balls of an identical colour – from the now hidden box.

The babies definitely looked longer at these balls when they were all white. Their observation of the mainly red box seemed to lead them to a sense of 'that's rather unlikely'. Their reaction was not about the colour itself; different variations of the same experiment showed that babies reacted with a long stare of surprise to five balls being picked of the minority colour in the box they had just seen.

Reflect for a moment on what this careful study shows of babies' thinking: their ability to look at their world and make a judgement about what is likely, and what is improbable. Their bodily reaction makes their thoughts visible, long before they can express their surprise in words.

Babies also seem to understand very simple addition and subtraction – not in terms of mathematical symbols but rather through events unfolding before their eyes. If there is one little toy on a tray and you add another one, then even babies of 5-6 months seem to expect that there should be two in total. They show surprise or stare if they are distracted momentarily and then see just the one toy. A similar baby logic of 'that's not right!' seems to work if there are two items, and you take one away – but by sleight of hand manage to have two items still there, or none at all.

It is also intriguing that some of this sleight of hand involves momentarily hiding the items from view. In other ways, babies of this age seem to operate as if something has gone forever if they can no longer see it. In some situations they stop searching for a hidden item, unless they are a couple of months older. There does not seem to be an easy answer

to this one – except that baby brains are more sophisticated than is often believed to be the case.

The power of play

The beginning of really early numeracy is intertwined with babies' growing understanding of the world around them: what is familiar and what is currently unfamiliar.

- Even very young babies show an awareness of what is well-known and what is new. Sometimes they will stare for

LOOKING CLOSELY AT ONES

Over her baby year, Tanith's ability to control her own physical movements worked alongside the experiences we brought to her.

- By the end of her third month, Tanith was making what looked like deliberate movements to connect with an item, such as bashing her teddy bear with her fist. Using eyes and hands she was more able to close the gap between herself and something interesting.

- In her fourth month, Tanith developed a clear pattern of grabbing hold of toys. Her grip was strong enough that she was soon able to shake her lighter rattles. By the end of the month she was keen to be held upright, securely on my lap and to enjoy the different views that this position gave her.

- Over the second half of her baby year, Tanith used her physical skills to get hold of, explore and play with a wide range of items. She liked any kind of sound-making toy, like rattles and bells.

- She enjoyed having items in bags and baskets, which she could explore with her hands and pull out in whatever order she wished. Sitting securely on her bottom and slightly bent legs, Tanith was able to use her hands freely for some serious exploration.

- Tanith loved bags and putting things in and out again. She put bits of Lego® into a box and then rattled them around. She did a lot of exploration about what would fit in what container.

- As she approached her first birthday, Tanith relished vigorous climbing over us, being chased by crawling, lots of tickling and cuddling. She discovered by direct physical engagement all the spatial relationships of over, under, through and on top of something or somebody.

longer at a visual sight that is new to them – although they do not tire of gazing at the familiar face of their parent or their key person in out-of-home care.

- Something familiar can be experienced by a baby as potentially interesting: worth reaching out to touch and grasp. Sometimes their facial expression and body language tells you, 'this may be interesting, but I'm not sure – so stay close to me'.

- Sometimes, a sight or sound sensation is too strong or sudden for this baby or young toddler and they show distress.

Even some practitioners, working with three- and four-year-olds, overlook how much young children are 'doing and thinking maths' through the flow of their chosen play and their involvement in daily routines like laying the table or tidying up play resources. In the middle of early childhood, adults are sometimes looking for something too complicated in terms of grasp of number. So it may require a serious adult 'stop-and-think' to consider babies' alertness to their world.

- Listen and watch out for babies when their reaction shows you they have noticed that one item has gone missing. They have a first idea of number or amount, in terms of what was there just a moment ago.

- Perhaps they have been momentarily distracted and, when they turn back, one of their collection of little containers has gone, or another little brush has joined their collection.

- Their sounds of surprise or a puzzled expression communicates the message that would be said out loud by: 'Hold on! There wasn't that many when I looked before!'.

- When toddlers start to speak, some of the early words are about amount–personal words like: 'nomore', 'allgone', 'onemore' and 'na'one'.

- Older babies and young toddlers often show enjoyment at the anticipation of physical fun that starts with 'one, two, three – go!'.

- Some young toddlers start to echo that pattern of sound in order to provoke a familiar adult into this happy exchange of being lifted up, gently swung or run-and-leap into your outstretched arms.

Babies or very young toddlers benefit from hearing number words in context. Familiar adults comment on what you and the baby can see: your shared focus of attention. As you sit on the grass together looking at the birds, you might say: "Ooh look", accompanied by pointing. You add, "There's a bird... Ooh there's another bird... over there... two birds". Mealtimes with older babies and young toddlers are appropriate times to ask: "I bet you can eat two carrot sticks".

Obviously, babies and toddlers do not do calculations or measurement as such. But they certainly do explorations and a lot of moving things about – following their own purposes. They try a lot of random bringing materials together and, until they have stockpiled relevant experience, a great deal of shove-it-and-see.

Soon you will observe the deliberate choice of familiar items, sometimes to bring them together with something less familiar, perhaps a new container. Then you see baby and toddler estimating and guess-estimating.

Some baby and toddler choices increasingly look as if they are based on previous experience. A confident reach and grasp communicates to a familiar adult: 'I know how to get a firm hold on this object'. The next action of an older baby or young toddler demonstrates 'this item will fit in here' or 'that item will make a satisfying clunk, especially if I can drop it'.

Hands-on experience of shape

Baby and toddler understanding of shape is led through their physical exploration of interesting three-dimensional objects which they can feel, lift, carry around, pile up and put into containers. They feel and see curves and edges. They explore what will fit inside and what will not, no matter how hard they push it. It will be a long time before toddlers, let alone babies, will make sense of the names given to different shapes. So long as they are not rushed along this learning journey, in time they will bring together their first-hand experience of three-and two-dimensional shapes with the correct descriptive words.

Babies' grasp of space is very direct. Space is experienced as a personal issue – cuddling up close so that there is no space between you or covering the intervening space at speed, by crawling or toddling in order to close that gap.

If you care for babies over the very early months you will notice that many can be uneasy or distressed if the open space around them looks 'too big and empty'. Prior to birth they have spent their life in an increasingly snug space. So it is not surprising that young babies often prefer to be wrapped or to feel the comforting boundaries of your arms. Some definitely like to feel the edge of a baby bath with their feet. Without this tangible edge to their world, babies may show a startle reaction of flinging up their hands and arms.

Babies need a rich array of safe materials that they can act upon and organise in ways that interest them today.

What works is very simple and some commercially produced toys are over-manufactured. For instance, babies and young toddlers are interested in shape as a quality to feel and they are keen to engage in a great deal of putting in and taking out. They also like to do a lot of what I call piling and filing

---

PARTNERSHIP WITH PARENTS: DOING IT AGAIN

Parents need to see developmentally appropriate practice with babies and toddlers in your provision and the key person can share anecdotes about individual babies. You need to share how simple play and 'doing it again and again' are the best ways to enable babies to explore their world and experience some basic mathematical concepts.

● Babies like placing objects or turning them around and looking, often with a steady stare, and from different angles.

● Older babies have the physical skills to put the same object in different places, try to make it fit into different containers and to drop or start to throw things, just to see what happens.

● Older babies and toddlers have a lot of fun with repetitive games in which you roll a ball away from you both. They crawl or totter after it, finding where the ball has gone this time and try to bring it back. You do it again, maybe at a different angle.

● Helpful adults tune into the importance of these repetitive games, noticing that each run of the game is not exactly the same.

● Ones and even rising twos need a playful adult assistant to keep this kind of game going. Even the older toddlers will be hit-or-miss with their ability to throw a ball, soft cube or other safe rolling or flying object.

– a very personal approach to organising and re-organising a generous supply of items that they can seize one at a time.

The problem with many commercially produced shape sorter toys aimed at under-twos is that the physical task of fitting up to five or six different three-dimensional shapes to the right hole is far too difficult for this age group. I have watched resourceful older babies and young toddlers with these toys. Whenever there is a lid to a posting box, they take it off and neatly simplify the task to fit their current skill level. The older baby or toddler then has a fine time putting any shape into the container, taking it out again, rattling the container with shapes inside, tipping them out again and so on. They are happy to use a simple lid with an all-purpose posting gap, into which a wide range of items can be eased. This age group is only ready to explore the simpler ideas of size around 'big' and 'little', along with a direct experience of 'too big', when something will not post through the gap.

Understanding the world

Like any other area of learning within the EYFS, your approach to 'Understanding the World' has to be securely grounded in the baby and toddler version of this kind of knowledge.

The world according to babies

You can only bring alive this strand of development if you envisage how well you might answer the imaginary question from a baby or young toddler of: 'Do you know and understand my world?' You have to start with what makes sense, what is familiar and important to this baby, toddler or young child.

Of course, as a key person to this baby you learn a great deal through partnership with their parents, and other family carers. Yet, you are also committed to getting involved in the intimate world of this baby: trying to see through their eyes and feel through their fingers – at least some of your time together.

Reflect on the following:

● What makes this baby's world different from that of another individual baby, even of a very similar age?

● Are you regularly, most of the time, at the level of a baby or young toddler?

● Do you know from direct physical experience what their world looks like from their position lying on their back, or on their stomach?

● Do you know what their familiar indoor and outdoor environment looks like from their standing height?

● Are there any changes you could make that would make a positive difference to them?

● Are you committed to understanding this toddler's world and his or her family life – important experiences that happen when they are elsewhere?

● How do you help with connections between parts of their personal world?

● Do they have a personal basket in which items from home, including laminated family photos can be easily accessible? Can they take photos home from their time with you?

Until babies are able to move themselves, you have to bring items of interest to them or take them in your arms to interesting sights. In a suitable physical environment for ones, they are able to see possibilities and eye-point them out to you, even before they can use the power of finger pointing. Babies are programmed to explore, to strive to use their physical skills, however limited those may seem within the early weeks and months. Neural connections within the brain are made when babies engage directly with their world using all their senses. They want to do or experience something again, and again, and again. Happy repetition is perfect for building those connections and for ensuring that practice makes better.

Sensory exploration and investigation

Of all the senses, smell is sometimes overlooked. However, like the other senses, smells are directly experienced by babies and the messages transmitted to their brain as electrical signals, like any other information they encounter in their world. Experience of smells, and their associations with people, routines and events, are logged in the infant brain, along with the associated feelings. It used to be thought that a sense of smell requires air and breathing. But there is now good reason to believe that in the womb a foetus reacts to different smells within the amniotic fluid. It seems that, like other senses, the sense of smell can operate in this liquid environment. Newborns are drawn towards the smell of breast milk. Part of their more general sense of familiarity with known adults is about how you smell (in the nicest possible way!) Smells soon become associated with other routines.

- Older babies often develop a strong attachment to an object, such as a muslin square, a blanket or a particular soft toy. The smell of this much-loved object is as important as how it looks and feels.

LOOKING CLOSELY AT ONES

- By 2-3 weeks old Tanith was showing sustained interest in objects within close visual range. She stared especially at a black and white panda cuddly toy, at lights and directly at the big eyes of a rag doll.

- Her interest in human faces led to some intent staring and by 7-weeks-old she was also intrigued by the face of the clock.

- During her third month, she looked intently at different objects: favourites were the pictures on her cloth cube, the dangling items on a cradle gym and one particular rattle that had a face on one side and mirror on the other side.

- Your only hope is to wash it regularly from the outset – which may not be possible, because a baby and then toddler will not let it go. Woe betide you if you wash it later, because you will remove the crucial smell.

- As I discovered, the exact feel can be just as important. I foolishly decided to mend the frayed corner of my toddler son's baby quilt, which had become his primary comfort object. His aghast expression, let alone the wails, let me know that I had ruined a key feature of the quilt. I had to unpick all my careful stitching and restore the corner to its tatty state.

Taste also seems to be activated in the womb and is an important sense from early infancy. Our sense of taste actually works together with the sense of smell. The taste buds on our tongue can distinguish four basic qualities: sweet, sour, bitter and salt. Any other tastes and subtle variations are detected by the receptors located high up in our nasal passage.

The sensory receptors in a baby's mouth are the most sensitive of all and they gain a great deal of information by mouthing objects. As well as any taste to an object, a baby's mouth also tells them about the feel, the texture of an object. It is a hopeless task to try to stop babies or toddlers putting items into their mouth; you just have to ensure that everything is safe. The sense of feeling, of touch, is activated as a foetus moves around, with steadily less space as the months go

Hearing also has become active before birth. There is plenty of support now for saying that babies can hear sounds from the outside while they are still in the womb. Newborns show an alert reaction to voices, like that of their mother, which they have heard many times. They also sometimes show a reaction of familiarity or reassurance to songs or music, which they have heard before birth. Human babies are poised to be attentive to the sounds of the human voice and the rhythm of spoken language. Around the world, they are soothed by singing and a musical sing-song quality to speech.

A suitable environment?

Babies are ready to find their immediate environment of great interest. The real world is fascinating; it does not have to be made more 'stimulating' for babies with commercial toys that increase the amount of random noise and create an artificial baby-world dominated by primary colours. The natural world is not dominated by bright red, blue, green and yellow. Look around outside; there are many shades, pastel as well as primary colours and so many different kinds of green or brown. A young child's world needs subtle shades and neutrals; then a few brighter colours will be of interest.

Babies do not benefit from being bombarded by bright colours. They benefit from having subtle shades and pastels in a physical environment that offers interest and contrast. However, their possible interest in black and white can also be overestimated. A myth has grown about the first year of life: that babies cannot see colours (untrue) and that they need significant levels of black-and-white contrast in toys to promote visual development and possibly also their brain development (also untrue). Please see Julian Grenier's article (2011) for a more detailed discussion of this issue. Babies have developed colour vision by two months of age, and some can distinguish colours at a matter of weeks

by. The importance of continued touch for newborns has been shown by how twin babies sometimes want to be close to each other. The physical presence of the stronger twin may reassure a baby sibling who still needs to be in the intensive care unit. Depending on the circumstances, medical staff may encourage the babies to be placed together, for at least some time, while an adult is beside the cot. However, the general advice on safety is not to place babies together in a cot to sleep, unless the adult is awake and observant. There is a risk that a physically active baby could roll on top of their sibling.

The sense of touch and being touched, often combines with the sense of movement. Babies often like to be rocked, perhaps accompanied by singing or gentle talk. They often like to feel the sensations of being on the move, walked around or in a pram or buggy. Over infancy, it will be many months before human babies manage any kind of independent mobility. It is possible that their most basic survival instinct tells them that being held close and moved means that they are safe and are not abandoned to the predators. In contrast with other mammals, human newborns are highly vulnerable.

Vision is operating as a sense from pre-birth and early infancy but a newborn's range for sharp focus is no more than the distance to the face of someone who is holding the baby in their arms. If you watch young babies you will see how they stare at objects and people who are within their clear visual range.

LOOKING CLOSELY AT ONES

- My own daughter, Tanith, certainly looked alert as a very young baby when she heard her brother's favourite rhymes and songs.

- More to the point, Tanith was hearing them again, since 'Miss Polly' and 'There was a cottage in the wood' would have travelled through to her many times before she was born.

- However, Tanith soon developed firm favourites of her own, as I tried out other songs I had learned from my consultancy work in day nurseries. By 3 months of age, her top favourite was 'Hello Aunt Jemima', which the practitioners told me was an old music hall song.

after birth. They see their world in considerably more than shades of grey. Babies enjoy some experiences of sharply contrasting black and white resources, including geometrical shapes. However, they neither need, nor benefit from, an environment that is predominately black and white.

Firm, moulded plastic as a material has become very common in many commercially produced toys for babies and young children. Babies lead their explorations through their senses. So, a major drawback to an environment dominated by plastic toys is that they offer an impoverished sensory experience to babies and young children. Plastic is a useful material when the alternative would be to use glass or china,

which would be easily broken by a baby or young toddler. However, plastic has minimal advantages as a general play resource and many disadvantages.

Plastic has limited interest by touch – it is smooth but cannot be bent or changed. It usually has no smell or taste/texture. Many such toys also have a visual overload, since so much is fixed to the basic resource. The appeal to sound is often overloaded as buttons release different pre-recorded noises, words or snatches of song. Furthermore, unlike a basket of ribbons or a collection of little boxes, it is not possible for babies or toddlers to get hold of one thing at a time, or a couple if they wish. They have no choice but to engage with the whole moulded plastic toy. For instance, they cannot remove the bit that does the bell so that they can explore the bell and ringing with intense baby concentration.

Exploring open-ended resources

Elinor Goldschmied, working also with Anita Hughes (2006), was a trailblazer for the value of open-ended play resources for babies and very young children. The development of the 'Treasure Basket' for babies, and the exploratory 'Heuristic Play' session for mobile toddlers, established a developmentally appropriate approach to resourcing the

LOOKING CLOSELY AT ONES

In the World of Discovery session, Jon (9 months) grasped with both hands a large square of dark cellophane. He pulled his hands back and forth, grasping on tight, and listened as the material made a rustling sound. Jon let it drop – the action looked deliberate – and then it picked it up again.

Then Jon rolled on the cellophane and wrapped himself up in it. From his face, it looked as if this had not been deliberate. However, Jon was not distressed (his mother was close by in any case). He just looked interested in what he had managed to do.

A younger baby lay on her back contentedly and held a large square of white organza – staring at the material, feeling it when it dropped to her face and experiencing the texture from her strong grasp on the edges.

In the second session, the children were mainly of toddler age and were able to explore the same array of materials as the previous group of babies.

- One really liked the dark net hanging curtains and played several rounds of peek-a-boo.

- Another little boy spent absorbed time with a length of black plastic chain and a large white bowl. He pulled the chain up to its full length – he was able to do this action because he was standing up – and dropped it into the bowl. The chain made a very satisfying rattling sound and he repeated this action several times.

- One toddler was held up by an adult so he could make contact with the pompoms suspended from the ceiling. He hit them and watched as they swung behind his head and then back round again. He repeated the action several times, looking fascinating by this movement.

LOOKING CLOSELY AT ONES

I was made welcome at a World of Discovery session at the Flagship Centre in Tilbury. This project across Thurrock offered the experience for babies and their parents to see and explore many open-ended resources.

Each session had a different array of materials. All the babies were happily absorbed for most of the hour-long session, some for the full amount of time. They were able to move around and find different items from the generous display available on the floor. All the babies spent some time on each item of their own choosing.

Their parents (In this session they were all mothers) and the session leader were present all the time and there was a soft background of quiet musical sounds.

The day that I visited, the resources were mainly black and white, but otherwise varied in size, feel and sound-making properties. This event is a good example of the point made on page 46 about black and white resources. There is good reason to enable babies and toddlers to focus sometimes on the contrasts of these colours. There is no evidence to support moves towards making black and white the main components of their usual physical environment.

environment for babies and very young children. Apart from babies' pressing need to be able to get their hands onto items of interest, their knowledge of the world rests upon being able to examine one bit at a time. It is difficult for babies to begin to understand the consequences of their actions – very simple cause and effect – if their play materials are too complex.

For instance, when babies can grasp and shake a little lidded tin with a cork inside, they are able to work out that the action of shaking causes the rattling noise. They may then experiment with dropping the tin and find that this action, done again and again, leads to a distinct noise. In contrast, babies cannot easily understand the consequences of their actions when their main play experience is from moulded plastic toys. A random lean one way or another may bring about a different noise, but the baby or toddler is less sure of the cause-and effect sequence.

The outdoors is a valuable source of open-ended resources and delightful experiences. The natural world does not need organising for babies and toddlers. They just need to get out into it with familiar adults, as in the examples described on page 25. The best safety equipment for babies and young toddlers outdoors is an alert adult, who watches out, but does not overreact.

Of course you need to ensure that babies and toddlers do not put earth and stones in their mouth. However, they can

be protected by gentle adult hands and still have the delight of learning about their outdoor world. They are interested to be held up to see the leaves or branches much closer than can be viewed from sitting or even toddler standing height. They will love to watch birds: in the trees of your garden, in the air or on the pond in your local park. They will be enchanted by real little creatures, whether it is squirrels or the local cats.

The curiosity of babies and young toddlers will be stimulated before they have the words for what they see, hear and safely touch. Yet their understanding of their world can, and should, start in the baby year – so long as their familiar adults enable them to see the outdoor and local sights. You comment simply on what you can both see. Very soon, older babies will be pointing out interesting sights to you and before you know it, they will start to use the words they have heard you say in a meaningful context.

WHAT ARE CHILDREN LEARNING?

I have placed my observations from the World of Discovery with the learning area of 'Knowledge of the World'. But the babies' explorations reveal other aspects of their personal development. Read through my observations of Kaylee (8 months) and reflect on what you would take away about her learning in other areas of development.

- She had a fine time with the cellophane. Kaylee was able to sit securely and she really pulled the cellophane about, making it rustle loudly. She waved it up and down, again and again vigorously, yet did not tip from her sitting position.

- Then Kaylee became interested in the base of the black and white box. She held it with one, and then two hands, then waved it around, dropped it and hit it.

- Kaylee then moved herself from the sitting position to get moving. She used a successful hump and pull strategy and got herself across the soft quilt covering to reach other items that had caught her eye.

- Over her time in the session, Kaylee spent her energy on a store of tissue paper, a black and white dumbbell shape that she could squeeze, rattle, hold, shake and squeeze again.

- She showed great interest in a laminated black and white pattern within a circle. Kaylee looked closely, shook and bent the laminated item. Then she held it firmly on each side and banged it against her legs, making a different sound.

Expressive arts and design

Creative development over very early childhood is only partly about exploration with arts and crafts, as enjoyable as those opportunities can be. This area of learning and development within the EYFS is about nurturing the flair of creativity in how even very young children approach flexible play resources and open-ended, first hand experiences.

Music and singing

The pleasure of music, sound making and dance are also included with this area of development. These experiences relate closely to the learning journey towards literacy, which is why you will also find discussion of songs and rhymes in that section. The rhythm of singing naturally links to dancing to music. Most babies like to be danced in your arms and a wise adult gets to know how energetically this baby likes to be jigged. Much like physical play, some babies like it very lively and others prefer a more gentle sway. Once babies are secure

on their feet and able to lean against a stable support like a table, some are keen to move to music by swaying themselves from side-to-side or up and down, by bending their knees.

Music needs to be used wisely as a resource. Young children do not benefit from non-stop background music. It just becomes sound wallpaper that children have to filter out in order to concentrate. The best approach is to choose different kinds of music and fit the likely mood of the time of day, having periods of each day without any music.

Babies and toddlers are very open-minded, enjoying a wide range of kinds of music. However, it is not true that certain kinds of classical music boosts babies' intelligence – the so-called 'Mozart Effect'. Wolfgang Amadeus Mozart wrote some excellent music and he can be one of your sources for European classical music. However, his music does not work IQ-magic anymore than an enjoyable CD from Celtic or South American traditions.

Hands-on creative exploration

Once babies are sitting securely, their hands are free and they love to explore natural materials like water or a thin, sploshy cornflour mix. Genuine creativity develops when young children are enabled to explore – fully supported by adults who ensure time for babies and toddlers to experiment.

You build firm foundations for young creativity by providing resources and appropriate tools and then letting babies and young children get their hands onto resources. You are nearby to keep them safe and show an interest.

- Young children need time to explore arts and crafts materials. For babies, the best tools are their hands and feet and they like to engage very directly with interesting materials.

- Young toddlers like simply to pick up materials and move them about. They need relaxed time to explore the properties of materials in their own way, with a familiar adult to ensure they are safe.

- Soon, toddlers will be more able and interested to use objects as printing tools. The shower scrunchy, feathers or twigs will be brought together with thick paint and large sheets of paper.

- Young toddlers start to explore soft play dough or other easy to manipulate mixtures. Again, their hands and fingers are their first tools and they like to squeeze, poke and push materials around.

LOOKING CLOSELY AT ONES

A joint singing time was the last event of the Rumpus Drop-in morning session. This was a small group of five children, toddlers and young twos, each with their parent or grandparent.

The singing time was active – paced but not too fast – with a brief gap between each song. There was always something visual to engage children as well as the actual singing. Lesley, the leader of the Drop-in, took the items out of a bag, one at a time.

The toddlers seemed to be especially enthused with the 'Sleepy bunnies' song, which they did several times with great enthusiasm. As I have seen in other settings, this song was definite hit with this very young age group. They clearly relished the contrast in the song between acting as the sleepy bunnies and then waking up and bouncing in a very lively fashion.

The great advantage of mixed age groups – whether in the home of a childminder or in group provision – is that young toddlers are increasingly interested in what slightly older children do with play resources. Sharp toddler observation skills and imitation are naturally part of early childhood. They watch how a slightly older child – friend or sibling – handles the play dough. Young toddlers can also join in cooking activities and they like to work with their own bit of bread dough. They observe what other children do, as you all make buns, biscuits or little cakes. It will not be long before these very young children want to make their own.

Creative thinking and exploration

Written examples of how young children think often start from the developmental stage at which they have sufficient vocabulary, and understanding of ways to use their language, to ask their own questions. Of course, babies and young toddlers cannot express their thoughts with spoken words. Yet, even young babies use their eyes, ears and physical skills to make sense of, and act upon, their personal world.

Hands-on exploration is dependent on the growing dexterity of babies and toddlers. Their strong curiosity and drive to discover provide powerful motivation to use their current skills and communicate with familiar adults when they need some help.

Babies, who have relaxed time for play and suitable open-ended resources, will try out ideas and repeat actions with their own variations. Babies will show you, by facial expression long before they have the words, what they are thinking. Older babies and young toddlers communicate feelings and thoughts that could be worded something like, 'yes, thought that would happen', 'now that is interesting, I wasn't expecting that' or 'hmm, need to try that one again'. Sometimes their expression and slightly tense posture tells you 'don't like that at all! Who made that happen?'. Babies may have created this situation by their action, but babies and toddlers have a limited understanding of cause-and-effect, even in their familiar world.

The focus in the EYFS on plenty of scope for genuinely child-initiated experiences applies to the whole age-range. The play resources for babies and young toddlers will not be exactly the same as for slightly older children, but they have much in common. In order for all young children to exercise choice, they need an attractive learning environment with plenty of accessible materials on open shelves and in containers. Babies will look (eye-point) to objects of interest and older babies will soon point with a hand or finger. Crawling babies will cross a room or outdoor surface to reach interesting resources and, like mobile toddlers, will often bring together play resources in a creative way.

Alert informal observation helps you to notice the flow of a child's creative enterprises, rather than impose adult reservations about 'proper play'. You need to focus on what actually interests this baby or young toddler today. For instance:

- Sitting babies will spend a long time focused, when they get their hands into a Treasure Basket or other container of interesting materials, such as a basket full of ribbons or scarves. The amount of time is surprising to practitioners or parents who say that 'babies can't concentrate'.

- Babies and toddlers puzzle things out in their personal world by getting hold of items, manipulating them and trying things out more than once and with slight variations of their own choosing.

- Toddlers will spend ages playing at making faces in a mirror, hiding and emerging from a large piece of material or finding out how the world looks through their legs.

- Look and listen to their discovery play. Let them see you enjoy watching and add a comment, if it seems appropriate.

Babies and young toddlers are keen to explore and try out what works in their world. Their open-mindedness gives them a head start in creative development and we need to ensure that our own concerns do not get in the way. Of course you need to keep them safe; babies and toddlers have no sense

PARTNERSHIP WITH PARENTS: BABIES AND THINKING

Older babies and young toddlers show you the power of their creative thinking when they act so as to amuse a familiar adult or children.

- In the second half of their first year, babies will often repeat an action that has made people laugh – one reason why you try very hard not to laugh the first time that babies blow out a raspberry sound accompanied by food.

- Mobile toddlers, who are can control deliberate physical actions, may repeat spontaneous clowning around when it has brought appreciative laughter.

- Young toddlers show a sense of humour, when they deliberately try to make everyone laugh again by the action that worked last time.

- It will be a long time before they can tell a conventional joke. However, some toddlers set out to amuse by saying something they know to be incorrect.

Reflect on the baby and toddler thinking power that lies behind endearing and amusing incidents. Long before they can put it into actual words, they show the ability to observe. They make causal connections between 'what I did' and 'how they reacted' and the intention to repeat that stream of meaningful sounds, those lively gestures or that funny walk.

of personal risk and actual danger. However, a safe enough indoor and outdoor environment will provide plenty of food for thought to nourish infant and toddler brains.

As much as possible, you want babies to be keen to find out for themselves: from when something does not quite go as planned just as when it has gone smoothly. Young children can develop as creative thinkers when they are allowed to make decisions in their play. Also, safety is not only physical; young children need to feel emotionally secure in order to flourish through their creative development.

The power of imagination

The development of 'pretend' is connected to the development of language over very early childhood, and with play behaviour in general. You are unlikely to observe very young children pretending in play unless they have reached the point when they use some recognisable words. Spoken language is itself a symbolic system: spoken words represent (stand for) familiar

PARTNERSHIP WITH PARENTS: BABIES AND THINKING

Toddlers start to exercise real imagination through brief actions. Their play then swiftly develops, so long as they have time to explore and plenty of open-ended play resources. Early years practitioners are important for recognising these early flashes of pretend play, and sharing anecdotes with parents, some of whom may be waiting for something more complex and extended.

● A toddler of 15-16 months may use a toy spoon to pretend to feed herself. You can see she is pretending, because it is not mealtime and she is chortling.

● Her actions and broad grin communicate, 'you know that I know that you know this is all just pretend!'.

● Toddlers pretend with resources that they see used in daily life, like speaking on the toy telephone. You support their imagination by joining in when invited to have a chat on the phone.

● Toddlers may create the 'vroom-vroom' noises for a car and 'fly' a toy aeroplane. Soon you will see that older toddlers can even pretend that a wooden block is a car and 'drive' it along with the correct noises.

people and objects. Pretending is a further example of this young child's ability to represent. The first pretend play actions are often brief. You can easily miss them, if you are not alert. An additional problem arises if practitioners, or parents, feel that play is not 'proper pretend' until you see the more lengthy three- and four-year-old version.

Very young children need to build a firm foundation of understanding how their world works. Their power of imagination rests upon, and leaps off, from what they have observed. So a great deal of early pretend play is woven around domestic routines and events. Toddlers often pretend to be doing something that they have observed a familiar adult do for real. You will most likely see the first signs of pretend within the second year of early childhood, but the emergence of this development is very variable. Some very young toddlers start not only to pretend in relation to themselves, but also move into imaginative play that involves other people or their toys.

Mobile toddlers benefit from contact with familiar, slightly older children who are at ease with the flow of pretend play. It is not unusual that three- or four-year-olds will invite younger friends or siblings into simple imaginative play. Toddlers and young twos are often tolerant of – they even welcome – being ordered about in roles they do not yet fully understand. It is a

By 13 months, Tanith enjoyed games with her brother (3yrs, 1mth). Drew did not want to play with his sister all the time. But he seemed genuinely to enjoy a lot of their joint games. He had actively developed these over the time that Tanith was an older baby and especially once she became a mobile young toddler.

● She was an active participant in a lot of chase and growling games with Drew and rescue scenarios led by his interest in sharks. They played together in the pretend house we had made from a very large cardboard box.

● By 15 months Tanith enjoyed being Drew's assistant in play. She sat and handed him Lego® as he made constructions that were beyond her ability.

● She imitated a lot of his pretend play, such as 'drinking' from a toy cup and 'feeding' from a toy spoon.

● By 15-16 months Tanith began to create her own games and play sequences. She would pick up her toy phone, give it to me with the indication that I should say something, and then take it back and 'talk' into the receiver.

● Tanith watched how Drew used the play dough and imitated how he used the rolling pin and shape cutters. She put little bits into the toy saucepan and offered them to me to 'eat'.

● By 19-20 months Tanith developed her own imaginative sequences involving dolls, playing with the tea set and pretend cooking with play dough. She also liked dressing up, although not necessarily as anyone in particular.

fair price to pay for being accepted into the company of the 'big' children. The benefit is that toddlers enjoy imaginative play that they would not yet be able to organise by themselves. The benefit for the slightly older children is that they have willing 'actors' for the minor roles in a scenario.

With their older child guides, toddlers can be active in the pretend shop or be chased by the (not too scary) monsters. In a friendly atmosphere, there can be a fair trade, so long as the slightly older children are not expected to accept toddlers all the time, or beyond the point when it is enjoyable. The observations in this section are from my own family. If you are a childminder, have you observed events like these in your own home? If you work in a group setting, do the different ages have the opportunity to come together on a regular basis?

Notes

Further resources

EYFS (2012) Statutory and guidance materials

The Department for Education website is a good one-stop shop for EYFS materials. See: www.education.gov.uk/schools/teachingandlearning/curriculum/a0068102/early-years-foundation-stage-eyfs

This site provides access to:

- Department for Education (2012) 'Statutory Framework for the Early Years Foundation Stage: Setting the Standards for Learning, Development and Care for Children from Birth to Five' – this is the statutory guidance, including the safeguarding and welfare requirements, which applies to all early years provision up to and including reception class.

- Early Education (2012) 'Development Matters in the Early Years Foundation Stage (EYFS)' – the non-statutory guidance explaining the four main themes of the EYFS and providing some developmental steps along the way towards the early learning goals.

- National Children's Bureau (2012) 'A Know How Guide: the EYFS Progress Check at Age Two' – non-statutory guidance to support this statutory assessment, to be undertaken by the key person/childminder in a two-year-old's early years provision.

Books and websites

- Arnold C. (2003) *Observing Harry: Child Development and Learning 0-5*, Open University Press.

- Beckmann Visual Publishing, *Baby It's you: the First Three Years* (DVD) (www.beckmanndirect.com).

- Blythe S. G. (2004) *The Well Balanced Child: Movement and Early Learning*, Hawthorn Press.

- Blythe S. G. (2008) *What Babies and Children Really Need: how Mothers and Fathers Can Nurture Children's Growth for Health and Well Being*, Hawthorn Press.

- British Heart Foundation National Centre (2011) 'UK Physical Activity Guidelines for Early Years' (Walkers) www.bhfactive.org.uk/homepage-resources-and-publications-item/280/index.html

- Campbell R. (1999) *Literacy from Home to School: Reading with Alice*, Trentham Books.

- Close R. 'Television and language development in the early years: a review of the literature' www.literacytrust.org.uk/Research/TV.html

- Community Playthings: 'Creating Places for Birth to Three: Room Layout and Equipment and other useful resources' on www.communityplaythings.co.uk

- Dorman H. and Dorman C. (2002) *The Social Toddler: Promoting Positive Behaviour* (book and DVD) The Children's Project www.childrensproject.co.uk

- Early Childhood Unit 'Everyday Stories: working with children under three' (www.everydaystories.org.uk).

- Early Education 'Learning Together' (www.early-education.org.uk).

- Featherstone, S. (ed) (2008) *Again, Again: Understanding Schemas in Young Children*, A&C Black.

- Gopnik A., Meltzoff A. and Kuhl P. (1999) *How Babies Think*, Weidenfeld and Nicolson.

- Gopnik A. (2009) The philosophical baby Bodley Head also a conversational feature on www.edge.org/3rd_culture/gopnik09/gopnik09_index.html

- Grenier J. (2011) 'Hue and Cry' *Nursery World* 1-14 November.

- Healy J. (2004) *Your Child's Growing Mind: brain development and learning from birth to adolescence*, Broadway.

- High/Scope UK (DVDs) *The High/Scope Approach for Under Threes:* www.high-scope.org.uk

- Hope S (2007) *A Nurturing Environment for Children up to Three*, London Borough of Islington.

- Hughes A. (2006) *Developing Play for the Under 3s: The Treasure Basket and Heuristic Play*, David Fulton.

- Jabadao, undated, *Developmental Movement Play* Jabadao: www.jabadao.org/?p=developmental.movement.play

- Jarman E, The *A place to talk series* (www.elizabethjarmanltd.co.uk).

Karmiloff-Smith A. (1994) *Baby it's You: a Unique Insight into the First Three Years of the Developing Baby*, Ebury Press.

Learning and Teaching Scotland (2010) *Pre-birth to Three: Positive Outcomes for Scotland's Children and Families*. www.ltscotland.org.uk/earlyyears/

Lindon J. (2006) 'A sofa full of talkers' In Featherstone S. (ed) *L is for Sheep: getting ready for phonics*, Featherstone Education.

Lindon J. (2009) *Parents as Partners: Positive Relationships in the Early Years*, Practical Pre-School Books.

Lindon J. (2010) *The Key Person Approach*, Practical Pre-School Books.

Lindon J. (2010) *Child-initiated Learning*, Practical Pre-School Books.

Lindon J. (2011) *Supporting Children's Social Development*, Practical Pre-School Books.

Lindon J. (2011) *Planning for Effective Early Learning*, Practical Pre-School Books.

Lindon J. (2011) *Too Safe for Their Own Good? Helping Children Learn about Risk and Life Skills*, National Children's Bureau.

Lindon J. (2012) *The Local Community: Planning for the Early Years*, Practical Pre-School Books.

Lindon J. (2012) *Safeguarding and Child Protection 0-8 years*, Hodder Education.

Lindon J. (2012) *Equality and Inclusion in Early Childhood*, Hodder Education.

Lindon J. (2012) *Understanding Children's Behaviour: Play, Development and Learning*, Hodder Education.

Lindon J. Kelman K. and Sharp A. (2008) *Play and Learning in the Early Years*, Practical Pre-School Books.

Manning-Morton J. and Thorp M. (2006) *Key Times: a Framework for Developing High Quality Provision for Children Under Three Years Old*, The Open University.

Moylett H. and Stewart N. (2012) *Understanding the Revised Early Years Foundation Stage*, Early Education.

Murray L. and Andrews L. (2000) *The Social Baby: Understanding Babies' Communication from Birth*, CP Publishing.

Oates J. (ed) (2007) *Attachment Relationships – Quality of Care for Young Children*, Bernard Van Leer Foundation (www.bernardvanleer.org).

Siren Films *Attachment in Practice, The Wonder Year, Firm Foundations for Early Literacy and Babies Outdoors*: www.sirenfilms.co.uk

White J. (2007) *Playing and Learning Outdoors – Making Provision for High Quality Experiences in the Outdoor Environment*, Routledge.

Zeedyk S. (2008) *Do Baby Buggies Affect Development?* (www.literacytrust.org.uk/talk_to_your_baby/news/1553_do_baby_buggies_affect_development).

Acknowledgements

I have learned a very great deal over the years from time spent with children, practitioners, parents, early years advisors and college tutors. I would especially like to thank the following people and places in connection with the ideas, expressed in this book.

My appreciation goes to Debbie Shepherd, 0-3s development officer, Thurrock and to the early years advisory teams of Derby, Coventry, Greenwich, Hounslow, Lewisham and Richmond.

Many thanks to these settings for their warm welcome: Buckingham's Nursery School (Leek); Grove House Infant and Toddler Centre (Southall); Mary Paterson Rumpus Drop-in (north London); Pound Park Children's Centre (Charlton, south London); Southlands Kindergarten and Crèche (Newcastle-under-Lyme); The Charlton Childminders Network (south London), The Flagship Centre (Sure Start Tilbury); The Rainbow Centre (Marham); I also appreciate what I learned working with Siren Films.

My thanks to the staff and parents of Grove House Infant and Toddler Centre, Little Rainbow Nursery, Mary Paterson Nursery School (Rumpus Drop-in), Robert Owen Children's Centre and Ecclesbourne Children's Centre for giving us permission to use the photos in this book.

I have changed the names of any children and adults in examples observed in actual settings. Drew and Tanith are my own (now adult) son and daughter and they have given permission for me to quote from the informal diaries I kept of their first five years. My thanks to Louise and Adam Gay who gave permission to use observations of Lucy and Sophie.